WINNING
THE JOB GAME

WINNING
THE JOB GAME

THE NEW RULES FOR
FINDING AND KEEPING
THE JOB YOU WANT

Carol Kleiman

John Wiley & Sons, Inc.

For general information on our other products and services please contact
our Customer Care Department within the U.S. at (800) 762-2974, outside
the United States at (317) 572-3993 or fax (317) 572-4002.

Wiley also publishes its books in a variety of electronic formats. Some
content that appears in print may not be available in electronic books.

ISBN 0-471-23525-3

To my children, Robert Kleiman, Raymond Kleiman Jr., and Catharine E. Bell; and to my grandchildren, Joseph Carroll Bell, Mia Elizabeth Kleiman, Carter Peterson Kleiman, and Raymond Kleiman 3d. The future is yours. Make it a good one.

And to Kathleen A. Welton, who makes good things happen.

CONTENTS

About the Author

Carol Kleiman is an award-winning columnist for *The Chicago Tribune*. Millions of readers nationwide look for Carol's three weekly columns on jobs and careers, "WorkLife," "Jobs," and "Letters," which are syndicated to more than 200 newspapers. With more than three decades' experience covering the workplace, she can help you be the one to get the job you want—or at least get a foothold in the field of your choice.

Carol is the author of critically acclaimed and best-selling books, *The 100 Best Jobs for the 1990s and Beyond, The Career Coach*, as well as *Getting a Job*. Her books have sold nearly 200,000 copies over the past 10 years. She has won numerous awards, including American Women in Radio and Television's award for her editorial commentary on *The Nightly Business Report*; outstanding columnist by the National Women's Political Caucus; Peter Lisagor award for business journalism; Midwest Women's Center Woman of Achievement; Illinois Associated Press award; United Press International award; and University of Missouri Penney award.

A nationally recognized speaker, Carol has appeared on numerous TV shows including *The Today Show, Sally Jesse*

Raphael, and *Oprah*. She has her own weekly TV show, *The Career Coach*, and she is a former commentator for the PBS program, *The Nightly Business Report*. *Newsweek* has called her "the Ann Landers of the job world," and *The New York Times* described her as "the undisputed godmother of workplace reporting."

ACKNOWLEDGMENTS

Even though writing is a solitary discipline, no author creates alone. I am particularly grateful for the support, assistance, and insights I've received while writing this book.

It was conceived and nurtured by Kathleen A. Welton, a brilliant editor, project manager, and friend. I deeply appreciate the professionalism, high ethical standards, and encouragement of Jean Nagger, my literary agent. And, of course, there would be no book at all without Michael Hamilton, senior editor at John Wiley & Sons, who immediately saw its timeliness and value and brought it to fruition.

My very special thanks go to Katherine Sopranos, my talented, loyal, and hardworking research assistant and friend who researched the best jobs and their salaries.

And I want to thank the following friends, family, and colleagues for their support (some of it involving rescuing my home computer!): Melissa Allison, Claudia Banks, Kevin J. Bell, David Birkenstein, Yvonne Bland, Meg Breslin, Tom Bridges, Greg Burns, Susan Chandler, Jim Coates, Terry Colby, Jean Davidson, Bridget Eckstein, Jamie Elich, Mary Elson, Terry Fencl, Melita Marie Garza, Dr. Anne Gordon, David Greising, Janice Jacobs, Rob Kaiser, Rob Karwath, Glenn Kaupert, Mary Jane Kleiman, Sally Peterson Kleiman, Angela Lee, Ann Marie Lipinski, John Lux, Walter F. Mahoney, Marilyn Miller,

Dr. Eileen Murphy, Ruthellyn Musil, Annie Noble, Marilyn Norehad, Teresa Parker, Daniel Paterno, Liz Peterson, Greg Prather, Hedy Ratner, Frances Roehm, Dr. Jadwiga Roguska-Kyts, Barbara Rose, Kate Rounds, Ilana Rovner, Donald C. Schiller, John Schmeltzer, Diann Smith, Karen Springen, Gloria Steinem, Darlene Gavron Stevens, Charles Storch, Shawn Taylor, Jack Thompson, Julie Truck, Stephen Viscusi, Maggie Walker, Tony Wilkins, Walter Wojtowicz, and Susan Zukrow.

THE 100 BEST JOBS

(Alphabetical Listing)

Accountants and Auditors
Actors, Producers, and Directors
Advertising, Marketing, Promotions, and Sales Managers
Animal Care and Service Workers
Arbitrators, Mediators, and Conciliators
Armed Forces
Artists
Automotive Service Technicians and Mechanics
Bill and Account Collectors
Biological and Medical Scientists
Broadcast and Sound Engineering Technicians and
     Radio Operators
Budget Analysts
Cardiology Technologists
Carpenters
Cashiers
Chefs, Cooks, and Food Preparation Workers
Chemists and Materials Scientists
Chief Information Officers
Child Care Workers

INTRODUCTION

There's an old cliché dating back to the 1930s that says a recession is when two or more of your friends lose their jobs but a depression is when you lose yours. And not just because just the thought of having to find a new job can be depressing. It's because times are bleak.

Of course, those definitions aren't your only barometer of the labor market. There are other indications, too, that times are not as good for job seekers as they once were. In addition to layoffs, companies are very slow to advertise job openings and even slower to hire.

Unemployment claims are the highest since 1991, and the weak job market is expected to deteriorate still further. It is taking longer to find jobs and they are paying less. The get-rich-quick promise of start-up e-business is down the drain, and those once glamorous high-tech jobs are getting harder to find. Even MBAs, the darlings of the business world with their high ambitions and high salaries, aren't being snapped up as they once were.

Employers in almost every field were hit hard, as we all were, by the events of September 11, 2001. Job seekers and jobholders alike were put on alert in October 2001, one month after the attacks on the United States, when unemployment soared to 5.4 percent and 415,000 jobs were lost—the biggest one-month jump in more than two decades.

Depressing employment news quickly followed, with dire predictions that the possible recession would be very deep and long, further deterioration of employment might be on the horizon, and that perhaps the economy wouldn't recover much even after the recession ended. These are the implications of today's slowing economy and labor market.

But the picture is not completely a grim one. There are still jobs out there to be filled, work to be done, and careers to be launched. And the fact remains that even during that gloomy October 2001, 94.6 percent of all U.S. workers—142,303,000 people—still had jobs. Today, everyone is going about the business of doing business, and trained and capable employees are needed in almost every area of the economy.

Whatever way the economy plays out, taking an upward bounce or a downward spiral, what you have to focus on and even hold on to at this point is that it takes work to find work, to keep a job, and to advance in your career—and that you can do it. There always are good jobs available. You just have to apply some elbow grease to learn where they are and how to get them.

Because these are such uncertain times, it's up to you to maintain the courage and stamina to move beyond the chaos and get and keep a job in which you can contribute your skills and know-how and be rewarded for what you have to offer.

POSITIVE TRENDS THAT AFFECT YOUR JOB HUNT

Despite the many negatives, there are significant positive trends operating in your favor. Remember all those Baby Boomers, who bore the brunt of so many jokes and so much derision, the 80 million Americans born between 1944 and 1960? Well, they're edging closer to retirement age—which means there will be more job opportunities for their younger colleagues.

Not only are Baby Boomers aging gracefully and leaving the workforce, they did you another favor. They had far fewer children than their parents did, which also reduces the numbers of those in the labor market. The children of Baby

Boomers, most of them now in the paid labor force, are called Generation X. It's estimated that Gen Xers (who also bear their share of late-night-TV jabs), those Americans born between 1961 and 1980, number only about 52 million—a statistic that leads some economists to conclude, despite layoffs and downsizings, that there will be a severe labor shortage in the next decade.

In fact, the U.S. Bureau of Labor Statistics estimates that by the year 2008 there will be a gap of 6 million between the number of jobs available and employees to fill those jobs. And the shortage is expected to accelerate in the following decade—which is more good news for job seekers.

The newest generation on track is Generation Y. These are the estimated 29 million Americans born 1981 and on. Most of them already are in the job market, and many are recent college graduates. However, the numbers of Gen Yers aren't overwhelming—certainly not enough to preclude you from getting the job you want. And it's still true U.S. workers will change professions at least three times over their work lives and change jobs at least six times. The reasons: by choice, being fired, or because of new technology that makes you and your job obsolete in a nanosecond.

IT'S UP TO YOU

"Being out of a job sucks."

That's how one job seeker put it. It's true—but what happens next is up to you. Helping you to make yourself the most attractive job candidate or the fastest climber on the career ladder is where I come in. These challenges are ones I daily research, write about, and care about. At *The Chicago Tribune*, where I've written my nationally syndicated "Jobs" column since 1983, I have my finger on the pulse of employment. I know from my daily contacts with job seekers, jobholders, and even employers that the employment market is a somewhat secret, even mystical, 800-pound gorilla. But it doesn't have to be like that.

This book will show you how to find out where the jobs are, how to be the one who gets hired—and once on the job, how to move ahead. If you're currently employed, you probably are worried about keeping your job and concerned about layoffs or bankruptcies. These are valid concerns, but knowledge is power.

I can help you attain the information and the guidance you need to make the right moves. You may not feel this way now, but after reading my book, don't be surprised to find yourself as excited as I am about the labor market of the twenty-first century—and extremely eager to be a part of it.

HOW TO USE THIS BOOK

This book is written for both job seekers as well as those who are currently employed. I will help you learn how to find out what's going on in your profession and industry—and how to use that knowledge to your advantage. I'll also help you build your confidence. You will know what to expect in order to play the interview game, make a good impression, and land the job. And then I'll help you move up the career ladder and be the one who still has a job, no matter what happens to the economy.

Chapters 1 through 3 give you a leg up if you've recently lost your job by providing inside tips on where the jobs are, how to get them and how to deal with the changed—and changing—job market. Chapters 4 and 5 show you how to keep your present job and how to advance your career. Chapter 6 emphasizes the importance of credentials, degrees, and lifelong learning in getting and keeping a job that's right for you. Chapter 7 emphasizes the importance of having not only a job but also a life, and shows you how to get a grip on both.

You Can Do It

Read this book from beginning to end or just the chapters that will help you most at this time. And when you're finished, you'll be able to go out and conquer the world.

Chapter 8 includes more employment tips and a summary of how to get and keep a job. Chapters 9 and 10 list the best jobs, their requirements, salaries, how many job openings there are, as well as inside tips. The material comes from the Bureau of Labor Statistics (U.S. Department of Labor's *Occupational Outlook Handbook* and America's CareerInfoNet). And an extra bonus: Each of the first eight chapters contains short paragraphs called "You Can Do It," an extra pat on the back and encouragement to make the work world work for you.

WINNING
THE JOB GAME

chapter 1

THERE *ARE* JOBS OUT THERE—
AND YOU CAN GET ONE

As you already know, most of the economic news today isn't encouraging for job seekers—but that doesn't mean you can't find a job. You can! Despite the drastic cutbacks and layoffs, which began early in 2001 and accelerated after September 11, workers still are needed in all the major professional categories. Employers still are hiring, and new areas of increases in employment emerge every day—such as defense manufacturing, military contractors, security and other protective services, real estate, health care, and pharmaceuticals, to name a few.

And even New York, which was hit hardest of all, is emerging from the terrorist destruction. Businesses affected by the horror are regrouping and reopening, if not in New York City then in nearby New Jersey and in New England states.

REAL JOBS FOR REAL PEOPLE

Despite the fact that our employment world has altered dramatically—many high-tech workers and financial wizards have been shocked to find their jobs eliminated—there are real jobs for real people. Information technology jobs, which rank among the five fastest-growing occupations, will stage a major comeback because they are the future of our economy, as were the manufacturing and agricultural jobs that preceded the current information age.

Yet computer-related jobs aren't the only ones with a promising future, though they seem to get the most attention because they often revolutionize not only the way we work but also our personal lives. Openings for the more familiar occupations will continue to grow as the economy regroups and recovers:

- Building custodians.
- Cashiers.
- Construction workers.
- Mechanics.
- Paralegals.
- Registered nurses.
- Salespeople.
- Secretaries.
- Teachers.
- Truck drivers.

THE STRUCTURE OF THE LABOR MARKET

Before you can even start looking for a job in today's challenging labor market, you have to understand its structure. The economy is divided by the federal government into two sectors:

You Can Do It

You will be the one to get the job because you will be better informed than your competitors.

1. Service producing.

2. Goods producing.

The Service-Producing Sector

Let's look at service producing first, which is now in a decline but is expected to be the first to recover. It's expected to grow the fastest, add the most jobs, and account for virtually all of the job growth. This sector includes communications, public utilities, wholesale trade, retail trade, finance, insurance, real estate, government, and services. Now, here's where the analysis of the economy gets a little tricky.

Included in the service-producing sector is the services division, its largest section with the most jobs and the most opportunities. Though the similarities of "service producing" and "services division" can be confusing, what you need to know is that the U.S. Department of Labor projects industries in the service-producing sector as a whole will account for virtually all of the job growth to the year 2008.

Jobs in the services division, which I like to call "helping" professions, include:

- Automotive services.
- Business services.
- Educational services.
- Health services.
- Legal services.
- Personal services.
- Social services.

Most of the jobs available today require brains, not brawn. And one of them has your name on it.

The Goods-Producing Sector

This government grouping is made up of agriculture, forestry, fishing, mining, manufacturing, and construction. Jobs in this sector, except for construction, have continued to decline. That's not expected to change, although if the country continues in a war economy manufacturing certainly will grow.

In fact, manufacturing industries in the goods-producing sector that are expected to show some gains are international exports, miscellaneous plastic products, business forms, newspapers, chemicals, and commercial aircraft. Still, this sector is largely unpredictable because of the chaotic times we live in. Who would have ever predicted that manufacturers of American flags would have such a bonanza, or, more sadly, that suppliers of fire fighting equipment would have more business than they could ever handle?

THE FASTEST GROWING INDUSTRIES

The 10 U.S. industries expected to have the fastest wage and salary employment growth from 1998 to 2008 have been researched and analyzed by the U.S. Department of Labor. (See Table 1.1.) Their projections were released after the events of September 11, 2001, and the good news is they remain unchanged despite the economic upheavals since that date. The fact that zoological gardens is a fast-growing industry is good news for my son-in-law, Kevin J. Bell, who is CEO and director of the Lincoln Park Zoo in Chicago.

You Can Do It

Though jobs in most of the goods-producing sector are on a downward swing, there still are jobs available, so if this is the area that attracts you the most, don't write it off.

Table 1.1 The Best Industries

Industry	Percent Growth	New Jobs
Computer and data processing services	117%	1,872,000
Health services	67%	809,000
Residential care	57%	424,000
Management and public relations	45%	466,000
Personnel supply services	43%	1,393,000
Miscellaneous equipment rental and leasing	43%	111,000
Museums, botanical gardens, and zoological gardens	42%	39,000
Research and testing services	40%	247,000
Miscellaneous transportation services	40%	94,000
Securities and commodities brokers	40%	255,000

Source: Bureau of Labor Statistics. U.S. Department of Labor.

THE FASTEST GROWING OCCUPATIONS

The government also has analyzed the 10 occupations it expects to grow the fastest in the decade of 1998 to 2008. What's telling about the projections is they underscore the fact that manufacturing no longer is the leading light of the U.S. economy: All 10 occupations are in the service-producing sector. (See Table 1.2.)

Check out the industry you want to work in or already are employed in and see whether it's growing.

Table 1.2   The Fastest Growing Occupations

Industry	Percent Growth	New Jobs
Computer support specialists	102%	439,000
Systems analysts	94%	577,000
Database administrators	77%	67,000
Desktop publishing specialists	73%	19,000
Paralegals and legal assistants	62%	84,000
Personal and home health aides	58%	433,000
Medical assistants	58%	146,000
Social and human services assistants	53%	141,000
Physician assistants	48%	32,000

Source: Bureau of Labor Statistics. U.S. Department of Labor.

OCCUPATIONS WITH THE LARGEST JOB GROWTH

Here is a list of the 10 occupations with the largest anticipated job growth in real numbers rather than percentages:

- Cashiers.
- Computer support specialists.
- General managers and top executives.
- Office clerks (general).
- Personal care and home health aides.
- Registered nurses.
- Retail salespersons.
- Systems analysts.

You Can Do It

Check out the fastest growing occupations and see whether yours is one of them.

Check out the occupations with the largest job growth and see whether yours is one of them.

- Teacher assistants.
- Truck drivers (light and heavy).

EMPLOYMENT BY MAJOR OCCUPATIONAL GROUP

The government also lists jobs by major occupational groups. Table 1.3 shows how many people are expected to be working in the nine different occupational categories by the year 2008.

Table 1.3 Jobs by Major Occupational Group

Industry	Total Jobs by 2008
Executive, administrative, and managerial occupations	17,196,000
Professional specialties	25,145,000
Technicians and related support staffs	6,048,000
Marketing and sales	17,627,000
Administrative and clerical support staffs	26,659,000
Service occupations	26,401,000
Agriculture, forestry, fishing, and related work	4,506,000
Precision production, craft, and repair	16,871,000
Operators, fabricators, and laborers	20,341,000

Source: Bureau of Labor Statistics, U.S. Department of Labor.

Use these labor force projections to figure out how good your chances are to get the job of your choice.

Under this listing, three occupations analyzed are in the goods-producing sector.

THE FORT KNOX OF INFORMATION

Detailed information on the best jobs is available in Chapters 9 and 10—more helpful information from the Feds. The U.S. Department of Labor is the Fort Knox of information about employment. That's why I always pay attention to it—and you'd be wise to do the same. Its Bureau of Labor Statistics (BLS) summarizes the projected job picture from 1998 to 2008 as one in which employment will increase overall by 14 percent.

Though this growth rate is slower than the 17 percent growth from 1988 to 1998, what I want you to see is that even though the job market is tight, job opportunities are growing in many fields, not decreasing. The BLS emphasizes, however, that manufacturing jobs are projected to decrease by 89,000—yet productivity is expected to increase. Manufacturing has gone so high-tech that employers can do much more with much less.

The service-producing industries will account for virtually all of the job growth, and various occupations within them will provide excellent opportunities for employment:

- Health services, business services, social services, engineering, and management are expected to provide almost one of every two nonfarm wage and salary jobs.

- Professional specialty jobs will increase the fastest and add 5.3 million jobs by 2008.

- Service workers are expected to add 3.9 million jobs.

You Can Do It

Whether you're a highly skilled professional or an entry-level worker, there are jobs for you. But having an education is better.

- The latter two areas—one with the highest educational requirements and salaries and the other with the lowest—are expected to provide 45 percent of total projected job growth.

OTHER IMPORTANT INSIGHTS

Additional jobs expected to grow faster than the average are executive, administrative, and managerial positions; technicians and related technical support professionals; marketing and sales jobs. The area of administrative support, which includes those hardworking clericals, will grow more slowly than most other jobs and a bit slower than in the past. This projection reflects the power of office automation. Yet the point to be noted here is that support staff jobs will, indeed, grow.

If you're employed or looking for a job in precision production, craft, or repair work, or as an operator, fabricator or laborer, these jobs also will grow more slowly, reflecting not only the new technology but also changes in production methods and the overall decline in manufacturing.

MORE JOBS

Here are some more fields predicted to need new workers in the coming decade:

- Amusement and recreational services.
- Computer and data processing services.
- Day care services.
- Electronic computing equipment.
- Human resources management (this is good news because these are the folks who do the hiring).
- Management consulting services.
- Medical instruments and supplies.

- Miscellaneous electronic components.
- Office furniture and fixtures.
- Offices of physicians and osteopaths.
- Oil and gas field services.
- Optical and ophthalmic products.
- Outpatient health services and facilities.
- Partitions and fixtures.
- Pharmaceuticals.
- Radio and television communications equipment.
- Residential care.
- Semiconductors and related devices.
- Telephone apparatus.
- Temporary personnel services.
- X-ray and other electro-medical equipment.

And there's still more: The U.S. Department of Labor emphasizes there will be hearty growth for the following jobs:

- Cardiology technicians.
- Dental assistants.
- Dental hygienists.
- Engineering.
- Mathematical and natural science managers (yes, managers still are needed).
- Medical records technicians.
- Respiratory therapists.
- Sales agents.
- Securities, commodities, and financial service professionals (yes, there will be a stock market).
- Surgical technicians and technologists.

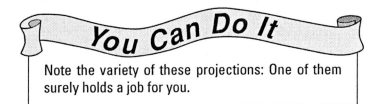

Note the variety of these projections: One of them surely holds a job for you.

OFFICIAL BUT ENCOURAGING PREDICTIONS

The government isn't the only entity carefully eyeing job opportunities. Economists, academicians, career consultants, and even Jobs columnists like me have their own ideas of what's out there. Though traditionally these groups disagree with one another and even themselves, some truths about today's job market are self-evident: Talented people still are needed in every profession, field, and job.

Now is the time for employers to hire from the cream of the crop. A study by Charles R. Greer, associate dean for graduate programs at Texas Christian University in Fort Worth, suggests the payoff for hiring in an uncertain labor market is high. Despite the fact that massive layoffs still are occurring in certain industries—I'll get to the bad news later—Dr. Greer notes that "companies that go against the grain and hire key managers and professionals during economic turndowns do better financially two years after the turndown." The reason: They have acquired high-quality talent.

Though the rate of job growth has slowed, industries that are "immune"—a word I really like to see and hear—to the current economic turndown, according to *The New York Times*, are health care, pharmaceuticals, education, mortgage banking, and security. And most of the current vacancies are in entry-level jobs.

As more and more retirement packages are offered and accepted, companies already are "starting to do selective hiring to fill in the holes," according to Jeffrey E. Christian, chairman and CEO of Christian & Timbers, an executive search firm based in Cleveland. The exit of older workers is especially evident among construction inspectors, secondary school teachers, and computing engineers, and finding qualified workers is a top priority.

You Can Do It

Job hunting is a numbers game, so make sure you know the numbers.

According to the National Association of Colleges and Employers based in Bethlehem, Pennsylvania, there are a few bright stars shining from East to West. Though employers hired 36 percent fewer new college graduates in 2001–2002 than they hired the previous year (the year before the start of the recession and the terrorist attacks), the good news, says Camille Luckenbaugh of the association, is that "government and nonprofit organizations project a 20.5 percent increase in college hiring." Traditional service workers such as hairstylists, cooks, and automotive mechanics will still be in demand, as anyone who needs a haircut, gets hungry at least three times a day, or owns a car can attest to.

THE WAR ECONOMY

Terrorism took on a whole new meaning after September 11 and had an immediate and direct effect on what was already a slowing labor market. But in the aftermath of the attacks, new demands created new opportunities that today shape employment hopes for many job seekers. While I firmly believe that good does *not* come out of evil, the fact remains that workers are needed to be part of the massive effort to defeat terrorists, protect American lives, and make sure daily life proceeds as normally as possible.

That's why jobs now are plentiful in the defense industry, which needs people with degrees in mathematics, engineering, physical science, and business as well as software engineers and financial analysts (to figure out all the new contracts, most of them with the federal government). The federal General Accounting Office (GAO) has announced that it is worried about retirements in the next few years of 45 percent of workers in the Departments of Defense, State, and Transportation, and in the Federal Emergency Management Agency. The GAO is so concerned that it even has suggested better pay and benefits, more active recruitment of young people, and cutting through the nightmare of red tape involved in hiring more personnel.

A quickly growing area (and some security-conscious people, particularly frequent fliers and workers such as flight attendants and pilots in the travel industry, wish it would grow even faster) is air safety. Late in 2001, an aviation security bill was passed authorizing the hiring and training of 28,000 new federal employees to screen passengers and baggage at all airports. Though the jobs are challenging and admittedly have an element of danger in them, if you're qualified now is the time to apply for one of these jobs because they include generous federal benefits and decent salaries for what used to be jobs with no status, no future, and high turnover. Screeners with private companies, for instance, who were paid on average $15,000 a year (if they lasted that long) are now being offered $30,000 to $35,000 annually.

The new law federalizing airport security is for three years only. Air marshals, too, will see an increase in job opportunities and salaries. And on the ground, hundreds of jobs now are open for firefighters, police officers, and emergency medical technicians. And what surprises me most of all are the numbers of people seeking and finding jobs at U.S. post offices, despite the bone-chilling anthrax scare. For instance, the U.S. Postal Service hired as many as 40,000 new workers for the Christmas season of 2001 and continues to hire.

And, in both the public and private sectors, computer experts who can counter cyberterrorism are having an easy time finding jobs. Additionally, bioterrorism has created an ongoing demand for medical researchers, chemists, physicians specializing in virulent diseases, and forensic specialists.

Though most experts label health care, education, and social work as "caring" professions—which they are—I add to that list security and safety personnel.

MORE INSIGHTS INTO REAL OPPORTUNITIES

Here are some promising job categories that have been revolutionized by technological inventions that have expanded rather than reduced job opportunities.

Health Care

Technology will create new opportunities for medical practitioners and technologists. Imaging machines already in use (anyone who has had an MRI—Magnetic Resonance Imaging—and has had to stay very still for what seems like a very long time knows how important they are in diagnosing diseases and injuries) will continue to be improved upon, providing instant color pictures of the interior of the human body. These machines already have revolutionized the health-care field and mean more jobs for nurses, other support staff, and technicians. Also in demand will be people who can design, manufacture, and repair new medical equipment.

Robotics

Though talk and much of the excitement about artificial intelligence have slowed considerably, particularly in the manufacturing of automobiles, it still is viewed as a viable and necessary tool, with new applications being researched and created by cost-conscious manufacturers and the medical profession.

Worldwide, engineers are creating robotic devices to do some of the detail work now done by humans, such as quality control and chemical analysis. An increase is anticipated in demand not only for engineers but also for technicians, electronic designers, robot installers, and highly skilled professionals who can build, service, and market robotic inventions.

Computer Graphics

Computer-Aided Design/Computer-Aided Manufacturing (CAD/CAM) and Computer-Aided Imaging (CAI) are rapidly changing the way visuals are created and transmitted, and if you've mastered these fields you will have no trouble finding a job. The two are used to automate the design and manufacture of products from industrial design to fashion to media illustrations, doing away with drawing boards, prototypes, scissors, and glue. CAI, which gives objects a three-dimension form, already has revolutionized entertainment outlets such as television, movies, and videos.

Information Technology

Because we rely so heavily on the latest information, whether at work or at home, the demand for workers capable of manipulating and analyzing data will increase. Continuing advances in microelectronics, fiber optics, and digital technology are creating jobs in storage, retrieval, analysis, and transmittal of information. Telecommunications, which includes the telephone, electronic mail, cable TV, computer networks, and satellites, will fill cyberspace with job opportunities in the coming decade.

Biotechnology

The study of biological diseases has become a must because of terrorist threats, as I have mentioned. Additionally, the application of biological systems to technical and industrial products and to solve medical mysteries are a new frontier for job opportunities, such as genetic engineering, human cloning, and solving human fertility problems, that will grow rapidly. Biologists and other scientists will be asked to better understand human and animal diseases, to produce better and safer drugs, to create disease-resistant crops, to neutralize pollutants, and even to devise microorganisms to extract oil from properties in the United States—and to do whatever else they can to diminish dependence on fuel from the volatile Middle East.

Lasers

There will be no letup in the strong demand for medical staff trained in the delicate microsurgery of laser medicine, which today fascinates a public grateful not to have to undergo

You Can Do It

Even in uncertain times, certain jobs continue to grow and new ones are created. Figure out where you fit in.

traditional surgery. Lasers will be used in a variety of ways—to speed up communication through fiber optics, to cut diamonds, to align underground pipes and sewers, and to speed up the publishing process. That means job opportunities will be plentiful for engineers, physicists, optical technologists, computer scientists, and technical and production workers.

A REALITY CHECK

Okay. Now you know most of the good news when it comes to employment growth. Unfortunately, there's more to the job picture than that. These are chaotic times, and in order to make sense of the confusion you also have to know where the job growth is slow—in other words, where the jobs are not.

In this way, you'll be able to make better choices and avoid unnecessary grief and frustration in your job hunt. As you already know, job cuts hit a 10-year high in 2001, and few experts are brave enough to predict what will happen next. Industries are changing to meet new market demands, which, of course, affects what kinds of workers are needed.

Though the service industry, as described at the beginning of this chapter, still is the largest segment of the current labor market, it was the hardest hit by the slowing economy and took an unusually heavy toll on people who usually are recession-proof: low-wage workers such as cooks, cabdrivers, cashiers, cleaning and maintenance workers, domestic workers, hotel workers, sales clerks, tailors, and that once always available refuge for the unemployed and actors and artists, waiters. Many Americans who had conquered the changes in welfare laws and had found jobs, albeit low-paying ones, once again are looking for work.

Professionals who are surprised to find themselves having to look very hard to find work are those who once worked for dot-com start-ups, for travel agencies, or as computer programmers, stockbrokers, general managers, sales supervisors, or marketing and advertising honchos. Unlike low-wage workers, however, some professionals took money and access to health-care insurance with them when they lost their jobs.

Manufacturing also has been on a skid, posting big losses because of disruptions and lost business from the terrorist attacks. As pointed out earlier, it has been on a decline for quite a while. I know this personally because I live in the Midwest, which once boasted of its industrial capabilities but has been known since the late 1980s as the Rust Bowl. Today, industrial output is going from bad to worse, and the decline is broad-based.

THE SLOWEST GROWING INDUSTRIES

Just as the federal government reports the good news, it also collects, analyzes, and distributes the bad news. Here is its list of the slowest growing industries and jobs:

- Blast furnaces and basic steel products.
- Compositors and typesetters.
- Crude petroleum.
- Electrical and electronic assembly.
- Footwear (except rubber and plastic).
- Iron and steel foundries.

You Can Do It

The current labor market is a far cry from what it was at the end of the century: It's now a buyer's market. But you can make employers want to buy you.

- Luggage, handbags, and leather products.

- Metal mining.

- Miscellaneous primary and secondary metals.

- Mobile homes.

- Natural gas and gas liquids.

- New conservation and development facilities.

- New farm housing, alterations, and additions.

- New gas utility and pipeline facilities.

- New local transit facilities.

- New nonbuilding facilities.

- New nonfarm housing.

- Private household workers (like manufacturing, on the decrease for more than two decades).

- Railroad equipment.

- Ship and boat building and repairing.

- Silverware and plated ware.

- Statistical clerks.

- Stenographers.

- Textile machine operators.

- Tobacco manufacturing.

- Watch, clock, jewelry, and furniture repair.

Though the job potential for many of these slow-growth industries seems grim, most still are hiring. They still have specialized and good job opportunities for those with the needed skills.

Additionally, plans to cut back on jobs are occurring in such industries as construction, nondurable goods manufacturing, transportation, and public utilities. And industries such as media, publishing, and business services are trimming the fat from their organizations.

THOSE MOST IN DEMAND

The professionals most in demand are computer engineers. They are needed everywhere, from financial institutions to manufacturing. Technology, though going through an unfamiliar period of downsizing in some areas, still is very much alive and well. The new technology is the future, and computer engineers, along with programmers, systems analysts, Web designers, and tech support staff, will lead us to it.

The semiprofessionals most in demand also are technicians but in a different way. This category includes:

- Administrative aides.
- Dental technicians.
- Educational assistants.
- Home health aides.
- Library technicians.
- Medical records technicians.
- Nurse technicians.
- Paralegals.
- Pharmacist technicians.
- Physical therapy aides.
- Physical therapy technicians.
- Physician assistants.
- Surgical technicians.
- Teacher aides.

The blue-collar worker is an unskilled or semiskilled worker holding a job that doesn't require advanced training or even a high school diploma—and these jobs are disappearing quickly because of technological advances: Remember when a garbage truck was filled not only with flies but with a crew of as many as four people? Now trash disposal is down to a one-person operator of a computerized truck.

Cleaning up and maintenance work are the mainstays of many blue-collar workers. The demand for janitors and cleaners is ongoing, as more and more of the baby boomers trade in their single-family homes for apartments in large buildings and high-rises, which need 24-hour cleaning and maintenance. But unless you have enough capital to start your own cleaning service, janitorial work, even where it is unionized, is not a career with a future, though it can be long-term. It's an entry-level job that offers low salaries, few benefits, and high turnover. But it still is a job that is much needed—and all jobs are dignified.

OTHER AREAS OF EMPLOYMENT

The federal government, no matter how much and how often it downsizes or freezes new hiring, is the country's largest employer, offering hundreds of different occupations and good benefits. The Department of Defense, even in peacetime, employs half of all federal employees. And Washington, D.C., isn't the only place federal employees work: Only a handful are located in the nation's capital, doing the nation's work.

So, don't forget Uncle Sam! State and municipal governments also are in the hiring mode, seeking police officers, firefighters, and prison guards. Though you don't have to be a brain surgeon to figure out that workers in private industry make more money and advance more rapidly than in the public sector, there's another benefit to working for the government at some level: You'll be making an important contribution to society. You will be helping others to live their daily lives a bit better—and you'll be giving something back, no matter what area you work in. Making sure parks are landscaped in the summertime and streets are clear in the winter are vital services. And you get all those holidays off!

Not-for-profit agencies also attract people who want to give back something in some way. The nonprofit sector is a magnet for people with intense beliefs and commitments. My daughter, Catharine Bell, combined her love of writing and animals in her first job out of college as a writer and photographer in the publications department of the Lincoln Park Zoo. "It was a dream job," says Cathy, now a freelance journalist and author specializing in the environment.

There are more than 1 million nonprofit agencies in the United States. They work in the areas of health, education, the environment, social welfare, religion, unions, arts, culture, community activism, social and fraternal organizations, and foundations. Pick something close to your heart and you'll find a nonprofit group active in it: They range from the Abbott and Costello Fan Club to Zonta International, and everything in between.

GEOGRAPHICAL FACTS OF LIFE

It's always been true that large U.S. cities tend to have more job opportunities than smaller, more rural, and geographically less accessible cities and towns. Studies show, though, that hiring was slow in 2002 in metropolitan area such as New York, San Francisco, Philadelphia, Houston, Seattle, and Chicago (where my son Robert Kleiman works; an event planner, party giver, and food and beverage expert, he is owner of Chase Entertainment).

In order to survive during economic turndowns, nonprofits, too, have had to be far more businesslike about the way they do business. The result is nonprofits also need people with business skills and are willing to pay them for their knowledge.

Brighter spots were Phoenix, Dallas, Miami, St. Louis, New Orleans, and Boston. The state of Hawaii, a beautiful place to live and visit, continues to have high unemployment. However, my son, Raymond Kleiman Jr., co-owner with Morgan Runyon of Runmanfilms.com, a documentary film company specializing in "rad" surfing movies, happily combines his love of surfing and movie making on the island of Kauai.

And don't forget that in a global economy, your job search doesn't have to be confined to the 50 states.

LABOR FORCE FACTS OF LIFE

Your competitors for jobs are expected to be quite different from a decade ago, according to the U.S. Department of Labor, because the composition of the population and workforce participation are expected to change. Here are some important facts to consider when you're trying to figure out what your best chances are to get a job:

- The labor force age 45 to 64 will grow over the period of 1998 to 2008 faster than any other age group as Baby Boomers continue to age. The labor force of workers 25 to 34 years old is projected to decline by 2.7 million—reflecting the decrease in births in the late 1960s and early 1970s.

- The labor force participation of women in nearly all age groups will continue to increase. Participation for men will remain fairly constant but is projected to contine to decline as the population shifts to older age groups that have lower employment rates. That means the number of women in the labor force will grow more rapidly than the number of men and will increase to 48 percent in 2008 from 46 percent in 1998.

- Asian and Hispanic participation in the labor force are projected to increase faster than other groups because of high immigration and higher than average birth rates. For Asians the increase is set at 40 percent; for Hispanics, 37 percent.

You Can Do It

Now is the time to pause to evaluate what you want to do, what kind of job makes you happy, where you want to work, and where you want to live. My strong suggestion is if it feels significant, important, and meaningful to you, do it.

- The African-American labor force is expected to grow less than Asian and Hispanic participation and is projected to be at 20 percent. It's noteworthy that the African-American labor force will increase twice as fast as the white labor force with its 10 percent projected growth rate.

- The Asian share of the labor force will increase to 6 percent from 5 percent and the Hispanic share to 13 percent from 10 percent. White non-Hispanics will see a decrease of their share of the labor market to 71 percent in 2008 from 74 percent in 1998.

- A radical change in the demographics of the U.S. workforce is that by 2008 the Hispanic labor force will be larger than the African-American labor force.

There *are* jobs: Now you are privy to the fact that there are jobs out there. The next step is exactly how to get them, and I will show you how in Chapter 2. You now have the grounding in what the employment market acts like and looks like, and you therefore are ready to take the next step in your job search: looking for a job.

chapter 2

PLAYING THE GAME

Most people don't look at getting a job as fun and games. And they're half right. It isn't fun. But there are some games involved, and in a volatile economy with fierce competition for jobs you have to be a number one player to succeed. Whether the economy is slow or robust, recovery near or far away, if you want a really good job you have to stand out as a highly qualified applicant.

There always has been a large field of applicants for the very best jobs. Now there is a large field of applicants for *all* jobs. Even those who do have jobs are concerned about current unemployment rates, an anxiety exacerbated, of course, by the terrorist attacks. Yet now is the time to exude confidence and energy in your job search—whether or not you really feel that way. It's the first step in "playing the game."

STARTING YOUR JOB HUNT

If you've been laid off—or what is euphemistically called "downsized" (whatever term is used it still means fired)—give yourself a little time to recover from the insult, but not too much time. I think a week to lick your wounds is plenty. If you can afford a brief vacation, now is the time to take one. Hope-

You Can Do It

Being unemployed in a volatile economy is a challenge. You have to keep your spirits up. My advice is to seek the support of family and friends, and indulge in chocolate bars and ice cream—and if I knew you better I might even suggest now is the time for lots of loving and affection.

fully, you'll return refreshed and ready to go after the prize. A job hunt is a 24/7 job.

If you stay home, try to relax and not think too much about what you will be doing next week. My theory about this period in your life is that if you stay home and become a couch potato propped in front of the TV set, you will soon realize that television was invented to get job seekers out of the house and looking for work. TV gets so boring and repetitious after a while that even a job hunt begins to look very attractive—the lesser of two evils, so to speak.

You Can Do It

If you feel you need a jump start in order to begin your job hunt, the U.S. government has a special toll-free hotline to help people who have lost their jobs. Its counselors offer referrals to free government services available to you and explain the various government training programs you can enroll in. The phone number for America's Workforce Network is 1-877-US-2JOBS. You may have to wait a while to get through, but learning patience early on is an important asset in your job hunt, which, I can guarantee you, will involve a lot of waiting.

SOURCES TO TAP INTO

Don't rule out professional counseling: It's worth whatever it costs. One-on-one counseling helps you figure out exactly what it is you want to do, because qualified professional counselors can help you cut through emotional roadblocks and clear the path for you to make the tough decisions about where you want to go and how to get there. Career and guidance counselors are skilled in guiding you to make choices about whether you want to look for a job that is easy to get that will feed you and your family—or if you want to take the risk of going after one you really love but that is harder to get.

To find a counselor, begin by asking friends and colleagues to recommend someone they have used and liked. If you're a college graduate, contact your school's placement center whether or not you've ever joined the alumni or paid dues. The school still has to help you. And their services usually are free to students and graduates because your tuition pays their salary. Plus, they usually have a job bank of real employers with real jobs.

Also check out the career guidance center of your local community college. Community colleges are supported by your taxes, which makes their counseling services relatively inexpensive. For the name of a private counselor, whose fees range from about $85 an hour up, call the National Board for Certified Counselors at 336-547-0607. Ask for a recommendation of a career counselor in your geographical location.

You Can Do It

Career advice is very helpful. I know. I give it all the time in my newspaper columns and readers really appreciate it. But don't let professional guidance delay your job search nor use it as an excuse to avoid beginning to look for work. After even one visit you should be ready to go, even if you continue your visits with the career counselor.

CONTINUING YOUR SEARCH

Also on your list of contacts should be the head of the university department you got your degree in. The department head—if she or he is doing the job right—frequently is contacted by employers (who often are other graduates) in your field who are looking for job candidates. If your college or university is in another city and has few listings in your geographical area, ask for names of alumni in your area, no matter what field they're in. Then, it's up to you to call them and ask whether they know about any openings anywhere.

I hear from many job seekers who get good job leads this way because alumni want to help each other out, all in the name of college spirit. Now is the time to call in all your chips with friends, relatives, and neighbors—anyone who might know of a job opening appropriate for you. Don't be shy about asking the people you pay money to for various services if they know of any opportunities. If they value you as a customer and client, they'll be glad to help. Asking around informally is a way of networking, and it can be very productive in a tight job market.

But one of the best ways to find out about jobs is through professional networks. If you belong to one in your field, access its job bank. Stand up at meetings and ask for help. Read the help wanted ads in publications of associations in your field.

JOB FAIRS AND JOB CLUBS

Job fairs are what I call "informational interviews sponsored by employers." At most of these fairs, it's rare that a job offer

Many people are reluctant to ask for help, but you won't get a job unless you do. You have to be proactive in your job hunt. No one can do it for you.

will be made on the spot, but you can learn a lot about the companies represented, make important contacts, leave your resume, and even set up a job interview. Job fairs are advertised in newspapers and often at Internet web sites. Look for them. Even if you're not interested in the jobs mentioned, if you want to know more about an employer that will have a booth there, go.

Be prepared for a job fair. It's very close to a job interview. Usually there are scores of employers represented, so first "case the joint" and decide which ones you want to talk to. Plan your day so that you visit everyone on your list. You can't accomplish anything in a haphazard way. Make sure you have a stack of business cards and your resume with you. Be as charming as possible to the various company representatives. A good word from them about you will go a long way in getting you the interview.

Job clubs are another form of networking. They also give support. They're composed of people like you who are looking for jobs. They usually meet once a week and are extremely effective in helping you to work hard at the job of job seeking. Because of group pressure, you will find yourself more determined to make all those phone calls, send out targeted resumes, and keep up on the latest information.

Job clubs are sponsored by libraries, community groups, religious organizations, schools, and state employment agencies. If you can't find one, form your own. Start with at least five other people who are looking for employment. Share information—but not about a specific job you're applying for. (If you don't get it, then you can tell the group about it.) The

Job seekers tell me that going to job fairs and belonging to a job club are two ways that build their self-images. And a positive self-image is what you need to complete your job search.

basic point of your own personal job club is that no one leaves it until the last person gets a job, no matter how long that may take.

INFORMATIONAL SERVICES

The nitty-gritty of a job hunt is doing your homework, finding out everything you can about the industry you're interested in, the companies that are hiring, what jobs are open, the salaries they pay, and the financial condition of the firms that interest you. Now is the time to make the first of many visits to your local library. Once again, don't feel embarrassed about asking for help. That's what librarians, the original search engines, are there for.

They'll help you find out all you need to know through books, annual reports, magazines, newspapers, stock market reports, professional publications, and, of course, the Internet. If you want to learn more about a particular job or industry you feel might interest you, contact the personnel department of one of the companies and ask for an informational interview.

If you know someone who works there, go that route. Remember, when you use the term "informational interview," the silent agreement between you and the company kind enough to open its doors to you is that you are not necessarily looking for a job; you're looking for information. So don't violate that promise during the interview. Wait awhile. Arrange, if you can, to spend an hour or so shadowing someone in a job you might want to do, seeing exactly what it entails and learning, while you're at it, what you can about the company. Don't stay too long.

At the end of the informational interview, it's okay to ask if you can contact the company sometime in the future; be sure to get the name, title, and phone number of the person who facilitated your visit and say how much you liked everything you saw and how much you'd like to work there someday.

If you've been granted an informational interview, you now have an important contact on the inside. Don't lose it. Write a thank-you note after your visit, and send your resume. Call in a few weeks to see whether you now can come in for a job interview.

TEMPORARY STAFFING FIRMS, EMPLOYMENT AGENCIES, AND HEADHUNTERS

Temporary agencies serve the purpose of placing you in jobs for what usually are relatively short periods of time but have the advantage of supplying you with income and a chance to continue your job search while employed. Even in chaotic times like these, when temporary employment has declined along with most other jobs, temporary employees who are skilled, flexible, and willing to work hard still are needed by shorthanded employers who want the work to get done.

As a temp, you work for the agency, which sends you out to various employers to fill in as needed. The positive aspects for you in this type of arrangement are that often a temporary job turns into a full-time one when you prove your worth; you get current experience to put on your resume; and usually the temporary agency will help train you and upgrade your skills, particularly your computer skills. The negatives are that work usually is not full-time, you have no control over the hours you work, there rarely are benefits or paid vacations, and wages are fairly low. Yet, it's my strong belief that it's better to have a job than not to have one—and I am not alone in that conviction.

An estimated 2 million people had temporary staffing jobs in 2001. Employment agencies place you in jobs offered by their paying clients, the employers. If they don't have a job you can fill, they don't try to find you one. That's not what they do. It's important to remember if you contact an employment agency that they don't work for you. They try to fill the job openings for the employer.

Frequently, I get complaints from job seekers who say they've been sent out by employment agencies to fill jobs they have absolutely no training for or interest in. Consequently, they don't last long. Another issue is the fee: Never pay a placement agency or a career marketer for a job. Interview only for jobs in which the employer pays the full fee.

Executive recruiters, also known as headhunters, work for companies that hire them to find qualified candidates for top-level jobs, usually with salaries of from $85,000 up annually. Recruiters, too, are hurting like everyone else in this economic downturn, but they still are the ones who get the prize jobs to fill.

Send your resume to recruiters in your field and follow up with a phone call. Remember that they, too, do not work for you. They work for the employers who pay them to find job candidates. If you don't get the job, they do not find you another one. Above all, don't answer their illegal questions, particularly those about your age. Still, it's important to be in their files and to keep in contact with them in case something comes up they feel they can recommend you for.

SMALL BUSINESSES

Before September 11, executive recruiters, staffing firms, and even temporary agencies had their plates full trying to fill jobs

If a headhunter calls you, whether for information about another job candidate or for a possible job opportunity for you, return the call immediately. Executive recruiters know where the best jobs are and what employers want, so if you are helpful to them they might be helpful to you.

for start-up companies, especially technology firms that absolutely guaranteed you would be a millionaire in a nanosecond if you came to work for their dot-com companies. Those days are gone, but start-ups are not, and they should not be ignored in your job hunt—not even dot-com companies, which have taken such a beating.

While large companies continue to lay off and do very careful hiring, small businesses—including start-up companies—still are the backbone of American industry. More people work for small businesses than for the 500 largest U.S. companies. You may have to be a risk taker to accept a job with a company that might not be around in a year (perhaps you already did that), but it might be worth doing to be part of a new enterprise that hopefully will grow. But I emphasize that in uncertain times it takes courage.

OH, THOSE WANT ADS!

I know you were wondering when I would ever get to help wanted ads, which are the first thing most job seekers turn to. I wanted to make sure that you knew all the other avenues of finding out about jobs before going to the ads, whether in newspapers or on the Internet. The truth is that more people get jobs through the want ads than in any other way.

It's not just because I work for a newspaper that I urge you to buy one—or two or three or four—papers every day, not just on Sundays, and read those help wanted ads carefully. If an ad looks promising in any way, clip it out and try to find out all you can about the job being offered and the company offering it.

Don't confine yourself to ads for your job title. Look at everything that may pertain to your field. You might fit in where you least expect to. A meeting planner I know was looking for a job recently, and after finding few meeting planner ads—a field hit hard by the events of September 11— he came upon a want ad for a catering manager. He had every skill required because so much of meeting planning is arranging for food, and he had the necessary experience. He got the job.

You Can Do It

Keep a file of the ads that you find that you think have potential and a record of what you have done in connection with them. That way you won't keep applying for the same job and will realize when an ad runs for weeks at a time that probably the company doesn't intend to hire anyone and that you should drop it from your file of possibilities.

Watch out for blind ads, however. The employers are very hard to track down, and you are completely at the mercy of the hiring officials because they know everything about you and you know nothing about them. I would try to avoid answering blind ads or sending your faxed resume to a number without a name or an address. If you're currently employed, even if you're on the verge of being downsized, you have to be very careful about answering a blind ad because it might have been placed by your present employer. And then, indeed, you'd be looking for a job for real and real soon.

ACING THE WEB SITES

The Internet can be daunting: There are so many job sites. I've tried to pare them down for you so that you're not over-whelmed and have come up with the 10 best web sites I recommend that you check out.

If you're not comfortable wending your way through the Internet, once again, stop in at your local library and ask for assistance. You'll get it. And if you don't have a computer, you can use the library's for your job search.

America's Job Bank. This is the most comprehensive Internet job site and resource center. It is maintained by the U.S. Department of Labor and coordinated by the 50 state employment agencies. It's first on my list because you can find jobs in your field and geographical location. Salaries often are included. And the federal Department of Labor and state employment services check to make sure the jobs are for real. They also make an effort to include only jobs that are current, unlike many other web sites. Access at: www.ajb.org.

CareerBuilder. It's a recruitment site that combines Headhunter.net and CareerBuilder's job search resources. The site is owned in part by Tribune Company. Access at: www.careerbuilder.com.

CareerJournal. From *The Wall Street Journal*, it features job postings ranging from executive and managerial to sales and marketing to finance and technology. Content includes news, features, and trends. Access at: www.career-journal.com.

Experience Works. This web site is America's largest provider of training and employment services for mature workers. Access at: www.experienceworks.org.

HotJobs. This is one of the largest one-stop career resource centers, with thousands of jobs posted by companies, staffing firms, and executive recruiters. Access at: www.hotjobs.com.

JobAccess. This site provides people with disabilities a dedicated resource to find employment and includes names of employers with real jobs for the disabled. Access at: www.jobaccess.org.

JobBankUSA. The job bank is an Internet recruiting site that provides job-hunting services to more than 5 million job seekers and employment professionals. Access at: www.jobbankusa.com.

TrueCareers. This is an Internet job search site from Sallie Mae designed to assist Sallie Mae's 7 million plus borrowers in advancing their careers. Access at: www.truecareers.com.

Manpower. The international staffing agency maintains a web site that connects job seekers with a range of employment opportunities. Access at: www.manpower.com.

You Can Do It

To play the Web game with skill, when you see a job listed at one of these sites that strongly appeals to you and also gives the name of the company doing the hiring, call up the company's web site and see if the job is listed there. If it is, apply for the job through the company's site. It will be more direct and you will have a better chance of getting a reply. Many job seekers report to me that the job listed on the company's own web site is substantially different from the one described in the virtual and mass job bank.

Monster. It's well named. It has more job postings than any other web site—and it's global. Jobs also are listed by geographic locations. Access at: www.monster.com.

WARNINGS ABOUT THE WEB

Thousands of job seekers post their own resumes on the various sites on the Internet and often are surprised not to get an immediate job offer. Though cyberspace is a vital area for job searches, it's not without problems—and you should be prepared for them. One of the main problems is that many of the resumes sent in response to jobs advertised are just that: only one of many. Often, there are so many that yours gets lost in the shuffle of the various companies' database junk files. Employers simply can't find you; in fact, they often don't even know you exist.

And more troubling is that some of the ads can be scams. Job seekers tell me they answer ads on the Web that seemingly are for jobs but when they go in for an interview they find themselves part of a crowd of other job seekers—and then the scam artists who placed the ad try to sign up everyone for expensive training programs that may or may not exist.

MORE CAUTIONARY TALES

The Internet is not a sure thing. Some experts even estimate that only 4 percent of those who post their resumes on Web job boards actually get jobs that way. And many job candidates complain when they submit a resume it sometimes is sold to other businesses and they are inundated with unwelcome mail and other correspondence that have nothing to do with finding a job. That's why I strongly recommend that if possible you instead apply directly through individual companies' web sites.

MAKING YOUR RESUME WORK FOR YOU

Your resume is the tool that gets you the job interview (see Chapter 3) that hopefully gets you the job. You need to set aside time to work on your resume very quietly and very seriously—but also with the understanding when you have finished that your work has just begun: A resume does not get you a job. What it does is open doors for you, so you have to prepare the most effective one you can.

In a fiercely competitive labor market, your resume is one of the most important tools in your game plan. Unfortunately, employers today get so many resumes they don't have time to read them all. You have to make yours the most readable, the most attractive, and the most seductive.

You Can Do It

Blindly sending out resumes in answer to newspaper ads or Internet postings is a waste of time. You have to know where your resume is going and how to tailor it to get you that all-important job interview. So your next step is to master the art of resume writing and submitting.

You Can Do It

Each resume has to be specifically tailored to each job you apply for. For the best results, gear it to a particular company and send it to a contact at the firm. Sending out scores of resumes each week may make you feel like you've accomplished something, but you haven't. You have to pick and choose where to send your resume: You want to increase your chances of getting a response by narrowing down your mailings and e-mailings.

ADDED VALUE

One of the benefits of creating your resume even before you start your job search is that it not only is a necessity in your hunt for employment, but it also gives you the opportunity to look at your work history, to acknowledge the skills you have and those you will need, and to absorb your work experience and educational attributes—in other words, to get a snapshot of what you have accomplished in the world of work.

Completing your resume may also precipitate some navel-gazing: What are your hopes for the future? Are you

You Can Do It

Sit down right now and start writing your resume. Do it on your personal computer, if you have one. That way you easily can switch items around, delete and add new information for each employer you contact. For your first draft, include absolutely everything you consider important. You can trim it down to one or two pages later. This time around, don't leave anything out.

proud of your achievements? How can you improve your life? Now is the time to think about the rest of your life, which begins at this very moment. Women who have annual health examinations—and hopefully all women do—know the value of a baseline mammogram: It's an essential measure of their health, a prototype against which future mammograms can be measured.

The same is true of your baseline resume: It's a prototype that must be created, updated annually, and used by you to measure growth, success, and, realistically, failure. And then it has to be adapted to whatever job you're seeking.

THE RESUME GAME

Human resource professionals are just as busy as everyone else, and their departments, too, are severely understaffed. So out of consideration for them and your own self-interest, try to make their lives easier and their reactions to you user-friendly by sending the kind of resume they want to receive.

Here's what employers tell me they want: Keep your resume as brief as possible. Hiring officers aren't interested in your personal life or activities. You can talk about them in the job interview your short resume will get you. Put the vital information, such as your title, accomplishments, and work experience, up front so that the reader can get it in one brief glance. And, as quickly and concisely as possible, include the names of former employers, your length of stay at each company, and your shining moments at each of them.

Employers rarely tell you this directly, but what they look for when they're in the hiring mode is easy access to your resume (which may be sent snail mail, e-mail, or fax); specific examples of your skills; your understanding of what the job they're offering entails; and how you can adapt what you've learned in previous jobs to the new one.

Meeting all these requirements as briefly as possible may be asking a lot of you, but it's important for you to ace the resume game to avoid having your resume tossed away before it's read. Pare it down to one page. Even on the Internet.

You Can Do It

Even though I call resume writing a "game," mostly to ease your anxiety about creating one, it really is serious business and not the time for tricks. Use plain white paper with your name, address, and phone number at the top if you send it by mail. If you e-mail or fax it, omit fancy decorations, images, bells, and whistles. Keep It Simple.

JUST THE FACTS, MA'AM AND SIR

Employers just want the facts. You can show your personality and even embellish your achievements in the job interview: A listing of where you worked and when, in chronological order starting with your most recent job, followed by your educational credentials is the Number One resume format for today's market. The chronological resume is the one I advise using. But the preferred resume doesn't work for everyone, especially people who have been out of the job market for long periods of time and those who have changed jobs frequently.

For the latter, a possible alternative is the functional resume. It prominently lists your skills, pertinent experience, and names of employers but omits the dates you worked for them. There is nothing devious about this form of resume, even if it isn't the most popular one. It gets the job done. And you can give more detailed information in the job interview, which you probably would not get if you sent in a chronological resume.

Another resume type—also not to be used unless absolutely necessary—is the historical, autobiographical, or anecdotal resume. It's really an informal way of talking about yourself and trying to attract the employer's interest. In letter form, write about yourself in the first person, emphasizing the details of your work life that qualify you for the job opening. Keep it friendly but as short as possible. Employers don't have time to read anything at length, even innovative resume forms.

All three forms of resumes—chronological, functional, and historical—can be used effectively on the Internet as well as for resumes sent through the mail or by fax.

THE TRUTH BE TOLD

While it's a sin to tell a lie under any circumstances, lying on your resume is the worst thing you can do. Not only is it wrong, but also you'll be found out. Smart employers—and you don't want to work for any other kind—carefully check out all job applicants they're interested in. They don't want to hire anyone with questionable characteristics, and they'll look into everything you say—remember, they're in no hurry to hire in uncertain economic times. They want to learn about your credit rating and police record and whether you pay your taxes. They may also find out that you do not have a master's degree in esoteric foreign languages as you claimed you do on your resume.

It's just as dangerous to put in phony employment dates to mask the fact that there are long gaps in your employment or that you have a tendency to job-hop. If you do so, you will be found out. I've been writing about careers for a long time, but I'm always surprised at the frequent letters, phone calls, and e-mails I get asking, "If I lie on my job application, will I get caught?" The answer is Yes.

There are other questions I'm asked, too, about resume reporting that are less obvious but still pertain to the same problem of hiding the truth. For instance, a common complaint I hear is that the job title held in the previous position doesn't cover all the work the job seeker actually did. The question: "Can I change my job title, which would be perfectly accurate to do, to fit in better with the job I'm seeking?" The answer is No. You have to give the official, real title you held in the job.

Otherwise, the discrepancy will be uncovered in a check of your facts and may cost you the job offer.

List the title you actually held but include all the job responsibilities it entailed that fit in with the job you're seeking. When you get the interview that your honest resume earned you, you can explain you had the same job responsibilities as those in the job you're applying for, but you didn't have the title.

Tired of being told she was "overqualified," a woman with a doctorate began omitting from her resume that she had a Ph.D. because it turned out, she says, to be a negative. When she removed it, she told me, employers began responding to her resume and for the first time offering her jobs. But she was very uncomfortable pretending she was less educated and wanted to know whether she "should continue this absurd fiction." The answer is No. I told her it was time to come clean but she might want to save her honesty for the job interview, when, if she didn't put the degree on her resume, she was obliged to mention it. I do think it's okay not to list degrees or credentials that aren't requirements for the job, but it doesn't take a doctorate to understand they have to be revealed in some way at some point. And I urged her to present proudly the information about her Ph.D. Continuous and continuing education is a must in today's labor market. (See Chapter 6.)

KEEPING YOUR RESUME FRESH

Job seekers, new hires, and long-term employees all have one thing in common: They must constantly revise, refresh, and

You Can Do It

Even though employers aren't always honest about what the job entails, what it pays, and even whether they actually are hiring, you have to be honest. Always. Set a good example for them.

A resume is an ongoing process, and you are the one who must make it go on.

update their resumes to keep them current. Even if you've just completed the Best Resume in the World, you can't tuck it away and forget about it. Resumes are the key to the door of opportunity and you constantly have to work on yours to make sure it's carefully honed. In that way you can add, when they happen and are fresh in your memory, important projects you've completed, new skills you've learned, awards you've won—and anything you may have omitted from your baseline resume that you know will make a difference in your job hunt.

BE PREPARED

In the worst-case scenario, which too many job seekers find themselves in today, you may lose your job. Instead of going daily to your regular work with its secure wages and benefits, you suddenly may be knocking on doors with one hand—and in the other you will need a current resume. While your competition, someone else who also was suddenly fired, may be at home struggling to come up with a viable resume, you will be ready.

In fact, you may get a job interview and a job before your competition manages to eke out a presentable resume. I often find it a struggle to convince placid, sometimes even smug job-holders, certain that nothing can ever happen to their jobs, that the time to update their resumes is when they're employed. My mantra doesn't seem to penetrate. Despite today's uncertain job market, which supervisory personnel surely know about firsthand, a study of 150 executives at the nation's 1,000 largest companies by Accountemps shows that 50 percent of the managers studied did not have an updated resume.

Make your resume the most frequently visited site on your personal computer and go to it even more often than you do to the games of Solitaire or Hearts.

Of course, 50 percent therefore did and were prepared for whatever comes next.

But learning that so many executives aren't facing reality is troubling. In recent years, middle managers have been among the first to be discharged when a company is going through an economic upheaval. Executives, of all personnel, have to be ready to go. Literally. Avoiding the issue of having a resume that works is a denial of current economic conditions that no worker at any level can afford to entertain. A "chaotic" and "volatile" labor market means just that: You could lose your job at any time for any reason.

THE COVER LETTER

As important as the resume is, you still have more work to do. Creating a succinct cover letter is a must. It's the bridge between what you have to offer and what the company wants. Its purpose is to make the hiring officer continue on and read your resume with interest. And the next step after that is your goal: being called in for a job interview. For years, I've asked employers which is more important to them, the resume or the cover letter. Most waffle on an answer and say both matter.

But when I question them further it becomes obvious that the cover letter is what makes them decide whether or not to read the resume itself. In a crowded field of applicants, the cover letter can make or break you: It's the first thing they see. And if it doesn't make you stand out from hundreds of other applicants, isn't impressive, or doesn't have any important facts in it, your resume probably will be deep-sixed. But if your

You Can Do It

In your cover letter, be sure to include a few words about something that you accomplished in your last job, such as a procedure you came up with that saved your boss money. And don't waste important space in the cover letter by saying how much you want to work for the company. They know that already.

cover letter attracts the interest of the human resources person or potential employer who is reading it, your attached resume will get the thorough reading it deserves. Many job seekers want to know whether a cover letter should be included when they send their resumes to a web site. The answer is Yes.

LINING UP YOUR REFERENCES

Now that you have your resume and cover letter in hand, you're almost ready for your first job interview. But there's one more bit of information you have to bring with you to the interview: your references. Listing the names, titles, and phone numbers of previous employers, colleagues, and other associates who know your work firsthand and who will present you in a good light and with enthusiasm doesn't happen by itself. You have to create your reference list yourself. Too many people just throw a list of names together without thinking about what they're doing. In these critical employment times, that's not good enough. Carefully select the people you want to speak for you. Talk to each of them and make sure they each want to be a reference for you.

EXIT STRATEGIES

If you're fired or laid off, try to leave with a written reference in hand. That way, you know exactly what the employer says

You Can Do It

When the people you choose to be your references agree to do it, ask exactly what they plan to say. Listen carefully. And then tell them what you want them to say. You can't leave this to chance. And make sure they understand how important it is for you to get the job. When a potential employer asks you for references and you give them, call the people involved and tell them to expect a phone call. Tell them about the company and the job you're applying for—and once again, tell them what you want them to say.

about you and it avoids a conversation between your previous boss and your new one, which can get sticky for you. Job seekers often tell me how much they hate their present job, their employer, and even the people they work with. They want to know whether it's okay during an exit interview or on their last day at that job to let everyone know exactly how they feel.

One accountant told me his previous boss, the one who fired him, "stinks as a manager." He wanted to tell him off on his last day purportedly "so that others might benefit from what I say." But he didn't fool me. He really wanted his revenge, which it seemed to me he actually was entitled to. However, my answer was a firm No!

It's not a good idea to burn your bridges. No one will believe what you say, anyway, because it sounds like sour grapes—and it will kill your chances for a reference. One thing you as an unemployed person cannot afford to do is to alienate a former employer you're almost certain your next employer will call for a reference. Bad references can destroy your job chances. Job seekers often suspect they might be getting bad references or that former employers are saying things that aren't true.

Readers tell me they have the right education and the right skills and still don't get the job. Yet the job remains

You Can Do It

With the right resume, cover letter, and now references, you're ready to tackle the job interview. In the next chapter I'll tell you exactly what to do and what pitfalls to avoid.

open. They wonder what they're doing wrong. Their problem may be the references that are being given about them. In some states, false reports of job activity are illegal and can be grounds for a lawsuit.

But when you suspect that bad references are costing you the jobs you want, how do you find out what former employers actually are saying about you—and whether they slander you to potential employers? You could start by calling your former employers and asking what they've said about you. You probably won't get an honest answer if they've unfairly bad-mouthed you. You also could talk to an employment lawyer about the matter, if you can afford one. (Don't consult management lawyers; they're not on your side.)

Another possibility is to contact Documented Reference Check, a company located in Diamond Bar, California. For a fee, it checks out your reference and finds out what's being said about you. Then it's up to you what to do with the information. "Some of our reports turn up vicious, malicious slander while other reports expose simple negligence in the human resources department," says Michael Rankin, the firm's chief service officer. "And you lose valuable job opportunities." Documented Reference Check has a free information kit, available by calling 1-800-742-3316. Its web site is www.badreferences.com.

chapter 3

BEING REALISTIC

t's the moment you've been waiting for: A potential employer has called you and asked you to set up a time to come in for an interview. Congratulations! I knew that you could do it and that you'd do well. Call back immediately and make the appointment for the next day, if possible. Asking to set up your interview within 24 hours shows your enthusiasm and interest in the job—and also increases your chances of being hired before your competition ever steps foot in the place.

You Can Do It

The job interview is a critical step in your job hunt. It's simply this: You either get the job or you don't. And the person who does best in the interview usually is the winner. You can be the winner by making the interview work for you.

THE JOB INTERVIEW

It's a tired cliché that you only get one chance to make a first impression, but job interviews were invented to illustrate that trite expression. In fact, most studies show that hiring decisions are made in the first five minutes of a job interview. I know that seems extremely unfair, but it's a fact of interviewing life and the way most personnel officers work. They go by a gut reaction to your personality, the way you present your skills, and your chances of blending in with an already established corporate culture—just as you have a gut reaction to the interviewer and the company, which you should also pay attention to. By knowing these parameters and preparing for them, you'll be fully armed for the interview and won't have too many surprises. You'll be ready from the first moment on.

One job seeker told me that she and the interviewer "clicked" immediately and that the interview after that was "surprisingly" short. But it shouldn't be a surprise that hiring officers make decisions quickly—and then it's just a matter of their assessing your skills.

BACK TO THE BOOKS

Since, in reality, your interview may not be the next day—you probably won't have it until the next week—you still have sufficient time to do a little bit more homework. Update your information about the company, focusing on the potential employer's goals and future plans. Try to establish contact with anyone you may know who works there to learn whatever you can about the person who will be interviewing you.

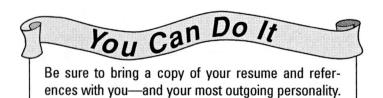

Be sure to bring a copy of your resume and references with you—and your most outgoing personality.

Busy hiring officers generally try to keep the first, yet most important, interview as brief as possible. Prepare to start selling yourself the moment it begins by being relaxed and, above all, friendly. It's time to whistle a little tune, prepare for some rejection—and to do a lot of work.

Another trip to the library at this point is a good idea. Don't be timid about enlisting the aid of librarians there: Your future job may depend on it. Organize the information you have about your own achievements and about the company. Study it—and plan in advance how you'll work it into your job interview in order to show how knowledgeable you are, that you're on the cutting edge of what's happening in the industry. If you know the company plans to open some new offices, you'll make the right impression by showing how well you're tuned in. Asking whether the job you're interviewing for might be for one of the new departments—and say how excited you would be to be part of a new enterprise.

GETTING READY

Study every item you so painstakingly put on your resume. Make sure you know every detail of every job you listed and when you worked there. You don't want to be taken by surprise when the interviewer asks, "When did you work at XYZ Auto Supply Store?" And you don't want to have to respond, "When did I do that?" Not in this job market.

When you are on top of what you've done, you can talk about it more easily. And talk is what you will have to do. Be prepared to tell anecdotes or stories about your past accomplishments, such as, "I saved my company hundreds of dollars just by reorganizing and updating our mailing lists. It was my own idea. No one asked me to do it but I could see it was

You Can Do It

What you actually are rehearsing is your sales pitch, and you are the product that's being marketed.

becoming more and more of a problem." Rehearse your story-telling with a family member or friend. The more comfortable you are with the facts you're presenting, the more impressed the interviewer will be with what you are saying.

MAKING A GOOD IMPRESSION

You have the facts, you have the spiel—you have the interview. Now you need to make sure you make a good first impression: You already know you only have a few moments in which to accomplish that. In a tight economy, the old clichés of what to wear to the interview are retro. They go back to the more formal way to dress for work of the 1980s: Your attire should be understated, not way out, not provocative. You want all attention to be focused on what you have to offer, not what you have to wear.

The secret is to look like the professional you are or want to be, even if you're applying for a job in information technology where sloppy dress and making Big Bucks in a nanosecond were once part of the job territory. But not anymore: Even though many companies have casual dress codes, usually for specific days or seasons, interviewers tell me they think it's disrespectful when job applicants turn up in jeans or other informal attire—even though they also admit you can probably wear whatever you want once you get the job. That's why, at the risk of sounding extremely conservative, I believe wearing business suits is the best bet for both women and men. I don't advise women to wear a dress, nor a suit with a low-cut blouse, nor a very short skirt. And I also advise women against wearing a pantsuit (which I live in; but then, I already have a job) sim-

For the job interview, which will take only a few hours of your time including getting there and returning home, remove all rings from your lips and nose. Take the ring out of your chin, too. You can put them back on after the interview.

ply because it's not traditional and may momentarily divert the interviewer from assessing your skills.

And you don't want an interviewer to be distracted. Men should look as if they're ready to go on a national television show, minus the heavy makeup: dark suit, white or blue shirt, plain tie, well-shined shoes. Both women and men should make sure their hair is neat; and women should go light on the makeup.

CASING THE JOINT

I know one job candidate who had an interview for a managerial position with a large supermarket, an area of retailing he hadn't worked in previously. He had no idea what to wear to the interview but came up with a creative solution: He stopped by the store a few days before his official appointment and saw that other store managers were wearing white shirts and dark pants. He wore that, too, but brought along a matching suit jacket. It made quite an impression on management when customers actually came up to him and asked him for information about where products were located!

Though the store eventually decided not to fill the position, a common occurrence in a slow economy, he was told he had made an excellent impression. Not only did he make himself more marketable, he didn't have to worry about whether he was wearing appropriate attire for the interview: He knew.

THE INTERVIEW BEGINS

You know you must be pretty good and have a lot to offer because you are the one who got the job interview out of an ocean of applicants. Get to the interview about 10 minutes early; you don't want to feel rushed. Before seeing the hiring officer, you may be asked to take some aptitude tests. Don't let this throw you. They're usually routine achievement or psychological tests. I used to advise job candidates to be very careful about tests and to ask a lot of questions before taking them. I don't do that anymore because jobs are too scarce. So just take them and do the best you can.

Obviously, the company is serious about you as a potential employee or they wouldn't bother to expend money to test you. When you're introduced to the hiring officer, shake hands firmly. Before the formal process of interviewing begins, it's okay to make small talk, which also has a purpose: It's a way to establish a connection between you and the person who decides your fate.

Sports, family, and the business world are okay to chitchat about. One woman told me she found out in the preinterview warm-up that both she and the interviewer were Soccer Moms—a fact that put both of them at ease. Politics is a no-no. Even if you were a volunteer vote counter in Florida during the Gore-Bush presidential contest and got a medal for your efforts, don't mention it.

But whatever you do choose to talk about, keep it brief. The interview is what counts, and you don't want to wear out your welcome. And you don't want to talk yourself out of a job. Hiring officers have told me that often candidates are so nervous they are guilty of being motormouths. They go on and on and eventually are in danger of talking themselves out of the job.

THE MARKETING OF YOU

From the beginning, it's up to you to be in charge of the interview. By that, I don't mean you control its direction by being pushy, aggressive, or obnoxious. I do mean that you have to

You Can Do It

Check that you have turned off your cell phone; if it rings during the interview, the hiring officer won't be amused. And put away your laptop computer and PalmPilot. In response to questions, always look the interviewer directly in the eye. You have nothing to hide. And sit up straight, just like your mother told you to so long ago. Remember, you want to give the impression that this is where you want to be. Nowhere else.

make sure you get in all the positives about yourself that you want the employer to know. That's what you've prepared for so long to do. Employers like to hire people who are excited, even passionate, about the job and the company. By showing from the get-go how interested and enthusiastic you are, you'll make a strong and positive impression on the interviewer in those all-important and decisive first few moments. It's called good chemistry.

SHOW AND TELL

Nonverbal communication counts, too. I often get calls from unsuccessful job applicants who are concerned they said the wrong thing in the job interview. That's possible, of course, but equally important to the goal of making a good impression are such things as body language, facial expression, your tone of voice, and your rate of speech. As Joan Smith, a career coach, puts it, "It's show, rather than only tell. Employers look for people who are energetic and command power." That's why it's important to speak slowly and distinctly and never to show any signs of subservience to the interviewer. By the latter, I don't mean that you should be arrogant or disrespectful; instead, show by your mannerisms that you are comfortable with the situation, and that you and the interviewer are two equal human beings getting together to help solve the problem of filling a job opening.

THE QUESTION OF QUESTIONS

Though some employers like to show that they have enormous power over you by asking you questions that make you extremely uncomfortable, most professional human resources people have a real and educated purpose in why they ask you questions and the way they ask them. Their goals are to find out what you know, to see how you respond to pressure and stress, and to get an inkling of what kind of character you have. As your career coach, I don't want you to be blindsided or caught unprepared in the job interview. To avoid that, I've compiled a list of questions that not only are the most commonly asked but also are the ones that often throw job applicants who haven't done their homework.

QUESTIONS YOU'LL HAVE TO HANDLE

The question asked most often—and usually for openers—is why you left your last job. Remember, it's not the facts that matter so much here, but that the interviewer is watching to see if you get flustered or on the defensive. Don't do either.

You Can Do It

No matter what the question is, even if you find it mildly offensive, show no other reaction to it than one of thoughtful consideration of the answer. Remain calm. Don't panic. Not being upset or put off by such questions is the best antidote to them. Whatever happens, you are showing that you will not fall apart. And it's a good time to work in all the positive things you want to say about yourself.

Sometimes it's worded differently. The interviewer will ask what went wrong in your last job to make you want to leave. To shake you up a bit, you might be asked why you were fired, even if you weren't. But the purpose remains the same. How do you handle the answer? If you were downsized or laid off, say so. They are legitimate reasons. If you were fired, never use that word. It will lead to too many questions you don't want to answer, so don't go there. And if you hated your boss, and vice versa, never mention that, either.

A job seeker told me how much he despised his boss and even his coworkers. And, he said, he had very good reasons for feeling that way. He wondered if he could talk about it in a job interview. The answer is no, never, absolutely not. A job interview is not the time to vent about how horrible your last job was.

Q. Why did you leave your last job? Did something go wrong?

A. No, nothing went wrong and actually I enjoyed what I was doing. But it was time for me to move on, to learn something new.

The next most frequently asked question, if it applies, concerns frequent job changes. Job-hopping is a red flag to employers, even in today's job market where the person interviewing you may have held three jobs in three years. What employers want is reassurance that after they go to all the trouble and expense of recruiting and training you, you'll stay on the job for the foreseeable future.

SOME MORE TYPICAL QUESTIONS

Here are some more questions you may be asked. Study the answers: You don't want to be perfect, but you also don't want to be tripped up.

You Can Do It

Employers still look for loyalty, even if they don't always give it in return.

Q. Do you consider yourself a team player?

A. Yes, I'm very proud of the fact that I am a team player. I know that when all members of the team work hard and do their part, the job gets done quickly and efficiently. I always feel very close to the members of my team. I rely on them and they rely on me. I get along well with people.

Q. Can you perform the task of . . . ? (The interviewer knowingly asks you about an area of business you have no experience in and which is not listed in the job requirements. The point is to see how flexible you are in handling the question and how open you are to new responsibilities.)

A. You know, that's something I've always wanted to learn. I've watched it in operation and am intrigued by it!

Q. Do you always tell your boss what she or he wants to hear?

A. I pride myself on being easy to get along with, but I also am proud of the fact I always answer my supervisors with honesty—and the facts to back it up—even if it may not be exactly what they expected to hear. I guess that makes me a risk taker, but I always do it in a professional manner and explain I'm trying to be helpful.

Q. Are you open to the idea of being transferred either from department to department or from city to city?

A. I certainly understand the importance of moving from department to department to learn more about the company and to advance my career. And I am completely open on the subject of relocation because I know it usually involves a promotion!

Q. You were in your last job for several years but you never got a promotion. Why didn't you get promoted? Was something the matter?

A. The company wasn't into giving new titles, but over the years I assumed a variety of new responsibilities. [list them.] Though handling new work and training new staffers weren't officially promotions, I did get frequent raises—which were another way of showing my added value to the company.

Q. The job you're applying for seems somewhat of a step backward for you, rather than forward.

It's work you've done before but at a lower level. Don't you feel you're overqualified for the job you're applying for? (This question frequently is asked of mature workers and is a subtle form of age discrimination, which I will refer to again later in this chapter. What it usually is getting at is that the company is concerned you will be a know-it-all and alienate other, younger workers. Also, it's the company's way of letting you know it will not pay you for your years of experience but only what it feels the job itself should pay.)

A. I know I have experience in this field—that's why I'm applying for the job. But even though I feel I can hit the ground running and do the work, I also know I'll be the new kid on the block and actually have a lot to learn. As always, I'll be as helpful as I can to everyone; and I hope they'll help me, too.

Q. Let's say someone in the department is cheating on his expenses, and has even bragged to you about it. What do you do? (This question isn't so much about your ethics as to see how you might handle a difficult situation.)

A. I would tell the person I find such behavior completely unacceptable. It is not a matter I would report to a supervisor because I feel it's actually none of my business. But I would let my coworker know I have my eye on him and am watching him closely.

Q. Your department is very late in filling orders. What would you do to solve the problem? (This is the type of question asked to see if you take responsibility for the work and if you are a problem solver. It's one of many questions you may be asked that are called "behavioral" questions: How do you behave in certain business situations?)

A. Even though I am not the manager, I would try to analyze the situation, see where the holdup is, and talk it over with my team members and other colleagues. When I have a handle on the problem, I would then ask to meet with my supervisors and discuss it with them. And here we go back to the question of whether I tell my managers things they don't want to hear. Yes, but in a very helpful way.

The previous questions give you some idea of what to expect in the area of your professional skills. Often, they're the easier part of the job interview.

PERSONAL QUESTIONS

It's critical for employers to know a little bit about you personally to ascertain whether you'll fit in. The personal questions usually come after the business ones listed so far. Today, interviewers are very skilled at asking in a way that reveals your character, personal life, and demeanor—the intangible qualities that tests don't show. The old saw about what book would you bring with you if you were going to be stuck on a desert island isn't used much these days. (The answer, of course, is a facetious one: a book on how to build a boat.) The questions asked in this category are far subtler, and your answers can reveal more about you than you may be aware of.

One of the trickiest questions is:

Is there something about you we should know?

One of the best answers is this: "I am extremely loyal, and loyalty, in fact, is a quality that is very important to me in both my professional and personal lives."

One of my favorite questions is:

What would you say is your greatest shortcoming? (Sometimes this one is preceded by "What is your greatest asset?" but they're more interested in your answer to this one.)

I would answer it this way: "I'm extremely well organized but I know I tend to work much too hard and too long. I even come in weekends and holidays to catch up with work. My greatest shortcoming, I think, is that I'm a workaholic."

One question is being asked with great frequency—and, I think, legitimacy—is:

How have the events of September 11 affected you both professionally and personally?

You Can Do It

Though a job interview is challenging, you're not going to be surprised by any of the questions because
you know what to expect. Freely answer the questions you feel the interviewer has the right to ask.
But only those questions.

Of course, only you can answer that question because sin-
cerity is key in this matter, but what is important to get across
here is that the terrorist attacks have made you understand
more clearly how much meaningful work matters to you,
which is why you are applying for this particular job, and how
important your family and friends are to you.

ILLEGAL QUESTIONS

Employers are crafty. They know how to ask questions that ba-
sically are illegal but are seemingly legitimate. It's all part of
playing the game. But this is one game you don't want to play
with them because you can't win it. Questions about your race,
religion, gender, age, marital status, national background, disabilities, sexual preference, health, height and weight, arrest
and conviction records, financial status, what type of discharge
you received from the military, and what organizations (including unions) you belong to are illegal in most cases, protected by city, county, state, and federal laws.

The rule is you don't answer such questions until a job offer is made because then it's okay to do so if you want to, and
it's even important for the employer to know the answers. Just
because a question should not be asked doesn't stop some employers. For instance, frequently they'll ask to see a driver's license even if the job doesn't entail driving of any kind. Why?
It shows your age, though the interviewer will tell you it's a
form of identification.

Being asked what year you graduated from college is

another ploy to determine your age. Give a general answer, such as in the 1980s or 1990s. Or just repeat where you went to college and what your degree is in. Asking your Social Security number opens the door to the answers to a lot of other questions. Job seekers often complain to me that they don't like to give that number out until they have the job. It amuses me as an avid social historian that when Social Security numbers first were introduced the promise was made they'd never be used for identification purposes. While it's not illegal to ask your Social Security number, it is illegal for employers to use it to check your credit or police record without telling you first and asking your permission. Employers also must ask your permission to get your financial history, if it's pertinent to the job. Employers must also tell you if credit information is being used as part or the hiring decision, so you have a chance to contact the credit service and make sure the report is correct.

Do you have to give the employer permission to check out your credit? Yes, if you want the job. But as I said before, employers know how to get around such obstacles as laws. While it's extremely offensive for a female applicant to be asked quite bluntly if she is "on the pill"—a question irate women job seekers tell me still is asked in some interviews—it is quite legal to inquire if you have any responsibilities outside work that might interfere with job requirements such as traveling. If you do have children or plan to, a good answer to that question is that while you are a responsible adult and take care of all personal matters in a seemly fashion, you also are a responsible employee and always get your job done.

You Can Do It

No matter how much the discriminatory questioning outrages you, don't let it show. Answer the legal questions professionally and state in response to the illegal ones that you'd rather wait until the job offer is made to discuss them.

NOW IT'S YOUR TURN

Most job seekers aren't aware that they are judged not only for the way they answer the interviewer's questions, but also for the questions they themselves ask. The best job interviews, even in a sluggish labor market, are those that create a two-way street of questions and answers: First you are asked all the pertinent questions; then it's time for you to ask yours.

Ask about things you really want to know:

- What is the exact job description?

- What is the grade level?

- To whom would you report?

- Is this is a newly created job?

If it's not new, and you feel comfortable enough with the interviewer to do so, ask why the previous person left and what you can do not to repeat that person's mistakes. But think twice before you ask because it's a loaded question—though an honest answer from the interviewer will be extremely helpful to you in landing the job. Ask about things you know the company wants you to care about:

- What are your chances for career advancement?

- What kind of training does the company provide?

- Is there tuition reimbursement?

- Are there annual performance reviews?

It's a good idea to make a list of questions before the interview, and it might even impress the interviewer when you take the list out to ask them.

- Does the company have plans for expansion?
- How is the company doing?

THE INTERVIEW WINDS DOWN

Your first interview is almost over and you now can breathe a sigh of relief, but not visibly! You prepared yourself well for the interview and did a good job. Now the interviewer is about to end it. Note, I've said nothing about salary or benefits (such as health insurance and flexible hours) or negotiations for them. They come up in the ensuing interviews, and there's not much to be gained from asking about them now. So hold off on these questions unless the interviewer brings them up. Remember, it's a buyer's market (the employer), not a seller's (you).

NITTY-GRITTY QUESTIONS

Right now, you have a very important question. And it's really okay and absolutely professional to ask it:

You Can Do It

Salary is often an issue that is a barrier to your being further considered for the opening. And you don't want to create any barriers at this point. So just wing any discussions of pay until the job offer is made. If you're asked what salary you expect to get, you should say you're completely open about the matter—even if you're not. If you're pushed hard, try to give a range, rather than specific figures. And, since you've done your homework about the job or asked the interviewer the salary grade for the job, you know what the range should be.

How did I do? Would you consider me for the job? I would really appreciate the feedback.

The best answer you can get is: "Yes, you did a great job and you'll hear from us soon." Second best is the detailing of some specific drawbacks to your getting the job. As hard as it is to listen to any of the negatives of your presentation, learning about them gives you the opportunity to respond to them while you're still there, under consideration, in the interview room. One job seeker told me the interviewer said he was impressed with her but her lack of knowledge of a particular computer program bothered him. Her instant reply: "I've never met a computer program I couldn't conquer. I'll start immediately to learn it."

Your next question:

What is the next step? May I call you in a few days if I don't hear from you?

The answer usually is yes.

TAKING LEAVE GRACEFULLY

Ask the interviewer for a business card and announce that you plan to follow up with a thank-you note and a phone call—and do both. Don't be embarrassed to state clearly and emphatically, "I'm very interested in the job. I want it. I think this company is great. I'll hope to hear from you very soon; if not, I'll be in touch with you."

HANDLING REJECTION

No matter how wonderfully the interview went or how certain you are that you got the job, don't count on it. Continue your

Employers are human, too, and it flatters them to know you want to work for them.

job search as if the interview never happened. You may have to go on several job interviews before you get an offer, so you can't afford to put all your eggs in one basket. You may not get the job you want because a better candidate might show up, the company might decide not to fill the job immediately, or it might even decide to save money by not filling the job at all. Maybe the CEO's son, daughter, or nephew was hired instead. Perhaps some of the facts on your resume didn't check out or your references were not what they should have been. Keep on looking.

Despite your hard work and best efforts, you might be rejected. Be prepared for it. Perhaps you simply didn't click with the interviewer or your skills weren't a match for the job. Maybe your credit rating scared off the employer. In all likelihood, you'll never know the real reason, so you just have to roll with the punches: It's a rough job market, as you well know by now, and job searches are taking much longer than they did a few years ago. Keep on looking.

When I ask employers how they can be so heartless as to leave job applicants hanging week after week and then so merciless as not to give any reasons for their being turned down, they usually respond that they prefer not to give any reasons at all because they don't want to be faced with lawsuits, either for alleged discrimination or for a verbal breach of contract. Another answer: They simply don't have time to reply to people they don't intend to hire.

BEING RESILIENT

You know all about bouncing back: You learned to do it when you lost your previous job. Being resilient is your best coping mechanism, a necessary skill in today's "new" economy. According to Elaine Chao, U.S. secretary of labor, during volatile economic times and upheavals in the job market, "it's important to maintain a sense of self-worth, confidence, and optimism." The old saying about what doesn't kill you makes you stronger applies here. You've learned a lot from your first job interview. Take a deep breath, be focused, and start all over

You Can Do It

It's perfectly natural to be disappointed. But don't spend too much of your valuable energy feeling sorry for yourself. Keep on keeping on.

again. You'll have better luck the next time—and even the times after that, too.

AND THE GOOD NEWS IS

If you got good news about your job interview and a request to come back for subsequent ones, start preparing for it now. In today's job market, I urge job seekers and job changers to take the first offer they get if it's even close to what they want. In the past, I urged job candidates not to take the first offer because it might be the wrong one for them. But, at least for the time being, I believe almost any job offer is right.

You want to get back into the world of paid work as quickly as possible. And having a job is the way to do it. However, in the days before the second (and possibly third and fourth, often with different people in the company) interview, take a few moments to ask yourself if this is a job you will be comfortable in:

- Do its ethics meet your own personal standard of conduct? (If you feel strongly that cigarette-smoking kills, or a loved one has developed lung cancer, you probably shouldn't take a job working in the tobacco industry.)

- Do you like the people you've met during your job interview?

- Will you be able to fit in?

- Do you think you will be fairly treated?

You Can Do It

Now's the time to be self-analytical and introspective. And when you make your decision, stick to it.

• Will you be able to move ahead and to earn more money?

SETTLING FOR LESS

Trying to find a job in an unsettled economy often means settling for less just to get your foot in that all-important door. Perhaps your concept of the right job includes annual bonuses, free cars, country club membership, and company support and programs to help you maintain a balance between your professional and personal lives (for more about the latter, which is a point you shouldn't have to compromise on, see Chapter 7). Of course, you deserve every single one of these things, but since employers no longer are relentlessly pursuing new talent, you may have to forgo most of them. Your values, interests, and ambitions are what make you the person you are; but some of them may have to be tempered just to get that job. Still, you don't want to work at least 40 hours a week at a job you think is meaningless—though being able to eat three times a day and pay your bills also has meaning.

What this adds up to is that during your subsequent interviews and negotiations for the job you've decided you want, you may have to compromise more than you'd like and settle for a lot less. You're not alone. Even those "obscenely paid" CEOs (the adjective to describe them comes from distinguished economist Graef S. Crystal) are acknowledging times are tough. Some of them actually are forgoing their executive pay for a year. Others are passing up on bonuses and stock options. Still more are including themselves in the salary freeze they've imposed on their employees. And another group is taking a pay reduction that ranges from 5 percent of their annual salary on up.

While negotiating a salary never is a level playing field—the employer has most of the leverage—there's even less equity today. You have to take what you can get. Recent studies show that job seekers sometimes are accepting salaries and titles that are less than what they expect.

NEGOTIATING FOR WHAT YOU MUST HAVE

The first interview usually determines whether you get the job. At least you know you have the interviewer's approval for the hiring process to continue. You might be interviewed by the people you'll be working with or run by top executives to get their okay. But what every interview now is about is the terms of your employment, particularly how much you will be paid. You can take that to the bank. If you have a minimum salary that you must have, state it clearly and stick by it. If health benefits are a must, make sure you get them. Anything more will be your "perks."

WALKING THE TALK

Don't let salary negotiations frustrate you—or at least don't let your frustration show. Part of your homework has been to check out the salaries in your profession and to find the company's salary range for the job. Listed in Chapters 9 and 10 are salaries

You Can Do It

Even though employers call the shots, you have a few things working in your favor: Companies usually want to fill the job as quickly as possible, recruitment is expensive, and employee retention a high priority. And, employers in the service-producing sector of the economy, which today includes most employers, know that customers are alienated and lost by constant employee turnover.

for the top 100 jobs. You can get a good idea of where you fit by studying those chapters for jobs in your field and for jobs in other fields that require the same skills and educational background as yours. As always, the U.S. Bureau of Labor Statistics has extremely accurate and useful salary information.

Other good sources for salary information can be found on the Internet:

salary.com. This is the best site, in my opinion. It provides various tools for detailed salary information, job title, geographic location, and market range. Access at: www.salary.com.

America's CareerInfoNet (ACINet). This is a comprehensive source of occupational and economic information that is part of America's Job Bank. Access at: www.ajb.org.

homestore.com. This web site helps you compare the cost of living in the United States and international cities. Access at: www.homestore.com.

You Can Do It

As you begin to talk about salary, you will understand why I earlier urged you not to give your current salary or the exact figure you expect to get in your next job, only a range. You would only be painting yourself into a corner. These facts are more than the hiring officer should know in advance and will adversely affect you. Employers prefer to know everything about your earnings without telling you what the job pays. That way, they can control salary negotiations and you will have no leverage at all. Don't play their game. Be creative about translating your well-honed skills into dollars—doing so can lead to a higher salary. Even MBAs, the darlings of the financial world, have to move very cautiously during salary negotiations, much like a porcupine with a graduate degree in business making love.

The Wall Street Journal Online. This online edition provides targeted salary information, including region, job title, and industry. Access at: www.wsj.com.

FINAL SALARY OFFER

When the company indicates it is making you a final salary offer, don't push too hard: Remember most companies are hurting financially, and so are you if you don't have a job. If you think you can live with the offer, that you have a chance to bump it up by good performance, take it. But take it without bellyaching—and get it in writing. However, to put the company on alert that you really think you should be getting more money, ask for a salary review to be held within six months. Tell them they'll have had a chance to see what you can do and might be more amenable to increasing your wages. You might get the increase you deserve at that time but you also might not: Employee raises are very small and more difficult to get in today's labor market. However, if the offer is too far below your expectations, say so. Make a counteroffer but be sure to explain why it is a valid one and the difference it will make to you. Not accepting the company's "final" offer may cost you the job but you didn't want it at that salary anyway.

MORE NEGOTIATIONS

Most job seekers dread negotiating the terms of their employment, but it is one of the most important tasks in the hiring process. Even managers, who often negotiate the deals with

You Can Do It

Though a salary is what you work for, getting a job, hopefully with benefits that could be worth thousands of dollars annually, is your goal at this point. Keep that in mind.

new hires, tell me they are very uncomfortable and nervous about negotiating their own arrangements. One of the problems is there is so much to think about: You have to ask about bonuses and incentives, time off, company-provided cell phones, insurance benefits, relocation pay, expense account reimbursement, subscriptions to publications you need for your job, retirement policies, and what flexible benefits are available for you to bring balance into your life. And as unpleasant as it is to raise the subject, you also have to know in advance about severance pay and benefits if you are terminated.

MATTERS TO CLEAN UP

Before the final job offer is made you probably will have to take and pass a physical examination. A drug test usually is part of that exam. You will have to pass both to get the job. And if you're still a smoker, now may be the time to give it up: Most businesses get healthy reductions in health, life, and fire insurance if employees don't smoke. If you do, it might cost you the job. And there might be something else the company wants from you before the job offer is final: a noncompete contract. This contract is a legal clause in an employment contract that says if you leave your job or are fired you can't work in the field for a specified time frame, usually three years, or in a certain geographical area.

Employers who insist on these contracts say they need them to protect their clients and their secrets. Employees say they take away their ability to earn a living in their profession.

You Can Do It

Ask friends, colleagues in the field, and members of your professional network what you can ask for and what you should get. Total compensation is the buzzword here—and you want your total to be as high as possible.

I say such clauses are an outrage. While I do agree employees should not steal company secrets or clients, in today's volatile economy, where more and more companies are closing their doors, a noncompete clause could mean that someone who lost a job after only three months on it couldn't work for anyone else in the field for at least three years.

More and more job seekers are rebelling against these agreements, and I say good for them. Since employers do want some kind of reassurance, for instance, that the new hire for their ad agency—which is losing clients by the dozens—isn't going to walk off with their remaining accounts, I think it's okay to sign a statement that you won't solicit company clients or disclose company secrets if you leave.

But that's all. An editor told me she was asked to sign a noncompete clause after being hired. She refused to sign, she quit, and the company eventually went under. She happily viewed these events from her catbird seat of an editorial position with another company. "I had worked in my field for 22 years," she said. "I wasn't about to jeopardize my chances to work in the only profession I follow."

Unions are good soldiers in this battle: They use their collective clout to try getting state legislatures to outlaw noncompete

You Can Do It

Just because you're presented with a noncompete contract, even as a condition of employment, it doesn't mean you have to sign it right away. Talk to an employment lawyer. Try to get the terms changed to ones that are acceptable to you. If you have to sign, then sign, but if eventually you do leave that job and plan to challenge the clause, increasingly the courts are ruling in the employee's favor. For legal information about noncompete clauses, I suggest you check out Carl Khalil's web site at www.break yournoncompete.com. Khalil is a corporate attorney and founder of Internet Legal Freedom.

You Can Do It

After you agree on a starting date that's okay for both you and the employer—asking to start the very next day probably is a little too ambitious, but very impressive—show how much you're a part of the team by suggesting you'd like to meet some of your new colleagues and to be shown around the office. If you're allowed to do that, it's a good idea not to hang around too long.

When you start your new job, you want to hit the ground running. Or, if you already are employed and want to make sure you're not the one downsized or "right-sized" when the next round of staff reductions occurs, in the next chapter I'll show you how to keep your job despite the challenges of an uncertain labor market.

clauses in certain contracts. Sometimes they succeed, as the American Federation of Television and Radio Artists did recently in Illinois for the broadcast talent it represents.

YOU'RE HIRED!

The job is yours. Congratulations! And to make sure everything is in perfect working order, get a written copy of your employment contract from the hiring officer. It should include your position, title, responsibilities, salary, start date, benefits, and everything else you discussed. If, for some reason, the company doesn't respond to your request, write a letter to the hiring officer with everything you understand that has been agreed upon. Give it to the officer and keep a copy for yourself. You don't want to find once you start a job that it's not at all what you were told it was—even the salary could be different— and a written contract will give you protection in court. An oral agreement counts, too, but it's harder to prove.

chapter 4

KEEPING THE JOB YOU HAVE

You've just landed a new job—enjoy your success! Or, if you are lucky enough to already have a job, enjoy your present status. You can never completely relax, though; eternal vigilance is the key to survival in today's job market. Think about the positives of your job. Before you start your new job or before you go to work today, create a plan to handle the responsibilities of your job. Perhaps you settled for less when you took it or perhaps you're settling for less by keeping it. But the fact is you do have a job and your office or plant will be the place you'll be spending long hours every day of the week. So before you even start working on how to keep your job, think a few moments about how you can be happy in it. It's up to you.

Being aware that you will change careers an average of four times over your work life and jobs possibly as often as 10 times (and that includes being fired or downsized) is the only incentive you need to take time to look long and hard at the basic requirements of your present job and how you will fulfill them. Realizing how well qualified you are for your job is a form of happiness—even if there are aspects to your job that you don't like.

Happiness may be a warm puppy, but in today's labor market it's also having a job.

MAKING LEMONADE FROM LEMONS

A woman who was laid off from her job as a bookkeeper when her employer went bankrupt (it wasn't her fault!) said she felt losing her job was a slap in the face, but, despite being shocked at her sudden job loss, she was determined to make the best of a bad situation. Her positive approach to being pink-slipped helped her get up and go, and within a relatively short period of time (only three months) she landed another job.

It wasn't exactly what she wanted. It didn't pay as much as the one she had before. But she knew that just getting her foot in the door of the new company was all she needed. "I'll prove myself so valuable," she told me, "that they'll want to keep me on and even pay me more." It's up to you to put the squeeze on those lemons you were handed. And a good way to approach your present job is to be in touch with your own needs and hopes and dreams, if not on a daily at least on a weekly basis. Examining yourself about the health of your present job will help you diagnose how close your work "temperature" is to "normal." Hopefully, it is close!

Questions to Ask Yourself

- What are the aspects of my job that appeal to me, that make me want to go to work each day?

- I like to feel I'm an important contributor. What do I accomplish each day that satisfies me?

- Now that I'm an insider, do I work for an ethical company, one I consider honorable?

- Am I being used to my fullest potential?

- While I know that salaries will be fairly low for the foreseeable future, can I live with—and on—what I'm making?

- If I do my present job well, will I be able to move ahead?

- Are my colleagues supportive? Do they include me in their conversations and get-togethers?

- Is this company open about its financial status? I don't want to get burned again.

- Is management aware I'm here? Do supervisors and executives go out of their way to say hello and make me feel welcome?

- Is my workload one I can handle?

If you answer yes to most of these questions, then your work "temperature" is healthy, and you also have a head start on succeeding in your job and holding on to it. But at this point, precise affirmative and negative responses are only a daily guide, not a permanent record of your strengths and weaknesses as reflected in your present job. Instead, the questions are ones you have to keep asking yourself on a regular basis so you constantly are in touch with how you really feel about your work life. They'll also clearly indicate to you how your employer feels about you.

You Can Do It

I believe all employees have the right to enjoy their work. Money matters, of course, but it's not all that matters. A positive attitude on your part can make your job a happy experience rather than a hellish one. It's up to you to create a good work environment for yourself—no one else can do it for you, or even wants to.

THE MEANING OF WORK

In the aftermath of terrorist attacks on the United States, many people began questioning their values and lifestyles. One theme I heard repeatedly, and still hear, is whether their work makes a difference. This self-analysis isn't a superficial indulgence in navel-gazing: It grows out of a need to spend our lives, our valuable lives, doing something that matters: Work needs to mean something. Proving to yourself and others that your life is of value doesn't, of course, make up for the lives lost in our recent national tragedies, but it is an excellent motivator for you to do your job well and to help you get up in the morning and go to work with enthusiasm.

AVOID THE AX

Being able to do your job well decreases your chances of getting fired when the economy, which seems to be on a roller coaster at times, gets tight. As devastating as it is to be fired, with the accompanying humiliation and other emotional downers, another unpleasant aspect of being let go because of poor performance or other insufficiencies should really give you pause: You can be denied unemployment compensation under certain circumstances. And sometimes, no matter what you do, you still may get the ax: Women and minorities still are the ones last hired and first fired. That hasn't changed.

WARNING SIGNS

Jobholders in today's labor market are training themselves to look for signs of danger. How can they tell whether their jobs are ones that possibly could be eliminated? Companies get in the layoff mode—the first thing executives do to save money, well before cutting their own perks or stock options, is reduce staff in a methodical way. There is nothing random about downsizing because the company still wants to be in a position to make money, and it does take a certain number of warm-bodied workers to do that.

But here are some things to think about in connection with your present job:

- Will you be replaced by a computer program?

- Do you work in a profit center of the company, rather than so-called soft departments such as public relations or human resources?

- How many people can do your job?

- Do your managers describe your work as "essential" to the company and tell you you're "indispensable"?

- Are your responsibilities increasing or decreasing?

- Do you bring in new business?

- Are you included in new projects?

WHAT EMPLOYERS WANT

I don't think the reverent (sic) Dr. Sigmund Freud ever asked the question, "What do employers want?" But he certainly should have. And employers certainly tell me that they want new hires to be able to be productive from the first day and for long-term employees to be productive for years. Here are some of their bottom-line requirements for employees new and old, and for good times and bad: Employers reiterate they want employees who are hard workers and problem solvers, and who are loyal, confident, committed to their jobs, easy to get along with, ambitious but not too ambitious, eager to learn, and flexible about their assignments. They don't want much, do they? Certainly not in their minds. And no one else's matters.

HIT THE GROUND RUNNING

Being able to hit the ground running means the company can continue moving forward without missing a beat—or losing money. In today' s job market, employers feel entitled to expect exactly that from workers. But I don't think even the most demanding employer expects you to nail the job on your very first day. Most give you some leeway and realistically expect a lag time with new hires, usually a three-to-six-month period of adjustment. The one thing you can't put on hold, though, is enthusiasm for the job. You have to show that from Day One, when you hit the ground running.

HOW TO KEEP YOUR JOB

Whether it's your first or 3,450th day on the job, here's what to do to make sure it's not your last:

- Be proactive about protecting your job. When appropriate, ask how you're doing.

- Have a personal strategy. Figure out where you want to go and then plan a way to get there, including your time frame.

- Be informed. Do your homework so if your department, company, or industry is in for bad times, you won't be caught by surprise.

- Add extra value to your company. Bring to the job—and use—skills not included in your job description. For instance, if you're a computer whiz, I, for one, would never fire you.

- Ask questions whenever you have them of colleagues and managers. And carefully watch everything going on around you.

- Stay competitive in your profession.

- Show flexibility at all times, from accepting new assignments in a positive manner to welcoming new employees and encouraging colleagues. And even if computer programs are a challenge for you, don't resist when new ones are introduced. Be smart: Embrace new technology.

- Be friendly with everyone, even people you don't like. It's not being hypocritical: It's being smart. Avoid cliques. Avoid backstabbing and vicious office gossip.

- You don't have to be best friends, but do be respectful of your team members. You can't get anything done without them. Your performance review and salary increases depend on how productive they are. Be there for them and they will be there for you.

- Avoid office politics, which are negative, but positively form friendships and alliances that advance your career without damaging anyone else's.

- Be part of the office grapevine or you'll miss out on valuable information. Use it as a power base. But don't participate in or even listen to anything destructive about your colleagues. (Know for sure that if you do, you are next.)

- Make yourself invaluable by offering to work whenever needed, volunteering for projects (especially management's favorite ones), and brainstorming with others to reduce bottlenecks.

- Avoid office romances. They're nothing but trouble. And one thing certain about them is that they are never a secret. Everyone knows immediately.

- Keep your sense of humor; it's better to laugh than to cry—even at the office.

- Don't ever feel your job is secure for a lifetime. It isn't.

You Can Do It

Read the employee handbook as if it were a bible. It is!

NOTHING TO COMPLAIN ABOUT

It's funny how a slowing economy and softening labor market reduce workers' complaints and shape employees' attitudes. In some miraculous way, tolerance for your job, your boss, your pay, and your working conditions arises. Employees who whine about not having enough storage space, too small an office, no assistant, office temperatures being too hot or too cold, boorish coworkers, or the "fact" that they are the only ones who ever do any work won't last in today's job market, even though they were tolerated in the tight labor market of the 1990s.

Steven Viscusi, president of The Viscusi Group, an executive search firm based in New York, warns against articulating such infantile complaints because your managers quickly will designate you a "high-maintenance employee." And since no one has time today to cater to your whims, you'll be among the first to be let go when there's a need to downsize.

In the years I've covered employment issues for *The Chicago Tribune*, I've built a reputation for being strongly pro-employee, which I am. That doesn't mean I'm anti-employer. I just feel employees need more support in what is a very unequal work relationship where the boss has all the power, unless you belong to a union. I've always encouraged employees to fight for their rights at every level, not to be pushed around, and to demand the respect they deserve. But now my advice is slightly tempered: I suggest you keep complaints to a minimum, to express and to act on them only when necessary.

When the economy goes on an upswing and workers are in short supply rather than so plentiful, it will be easier to speak up and demand your rights. And there will be more certainty that someone will listen to you, the first step before remedial action can be taken. One of the management techniques that outrages my sense of fair play is the invasion of employees' privacy by monitoring their phone calls, e-mail messages, faxes, and computer use and asking intrusive though legal questions on job applications. These are standard in most offices, and employees have to be aware of them. Employers say they have to invade workers' privacy because as employees they really have none. In addition, it's a way to check how many hours employees might be wasting doing things not connected with work. It's also a check on whether company secrets are being disclosed to others and whether ethical standards are being observed.

Despite my usual insistence that employees should be trusted and not spied on, I also believe that now is not the time to take action against employers, at least not by yourself. Legal rights, which go well beyond the category of complaining, must be protected at all times. I haven't changed my tune about that. But those rights in the gray areas and others that could cost you your job in a tight economy may have to be put on hold.

"I'm a fighter," a health care professional told me. "I don't take abuse too well. And I'm always there for others when they want to speak up about their rights. But right now I'm taking a hiatus. Instead, I'm devoting all my energy to getting my job done since I now do two people's work—the other person was fired. That doesn't mean I'm not aware of things I think unfair. I still go to bat if I think the causes are worthy. But if they're something I can live with for the short term, I think it's wise not to get too riled up about them. But just wait till the economy picks up!"

DO YOUR HOMEWORK

Research each problem thoroughly. Find out whether other employees are impacted or upset by the situation. And when you have all the facts collected and have some remedies to suggest,

You should never have to be in a position where you feel you're being abused, pushed around, or unfairly treated. But before speaking up or taking action against the indignities that have arisen and which seriously concern you, carefully think about them.

present them to your manager—but not in an accusing or confrontational way. That is counterproductive, even in good times. And don't do it alone. Bring one or two colleagues along. If no one else will speak up, it's a strong clue for you that you may have to wait to voice your objections.

Complaints about the Boss from Hell

Even in tough economic times, even when you think twice about complaining of indignities you wouldn't have tolerated for one minute when there were more jobs than people to fill them—don't allow yourself to be victimized by the Boss from Hell. Tyrants thrive when they're not opposed, and if you let yourself become the target of a neurotic or power-hungry manager, you soon may find yourself with falling productivity, rising stress, and anger that is out of this world. And out of a job.

Terrorist Tactics

Big Bad Bosses are easily identifiable: The one thing they have in common is that they relish making fun of you in front of your colleagues, gaining strength from your apparent weakness and guilt. The more defensive and apologetic you become, the stronger they feel they are. And when they "cut you down to size" in their smug and arrogant way, especially in front of your fellow workers, the happier they are. They feed on your insecurities, so if you are foolish enough to show even a smidgen of anxiety about their behavior, they'll work hard to exact a full yard of it from you.

Don't let your in-office terrorist intimidate you or ruin your career. Fight back, but in a professional way.

"My boss was a nightmare and always had it in for the newest person in the department," a clerk at an insurance company told me. "At first, when I was the new kid, I would get so upset that I cried in front of him. That didn't stop him. Soon I realized he wanted to get me upset, so I refused to let him see how much he upset me. Instead, I started to laugh out loud at his outbursts, as you would at a toddler with temper tantrums. It made me feel better and, believe it or not, he very quickly stopped picking on me." Not everyone has such success. "I yelled back at my boss when he yelled at me," a legal secretary told me. "You know how lawyers are and their enormous egos. Well, I didn't get fired but he did get me transferred to another department where people seem to be very wary of me. I think I have to start looking for another job."

Of course, inflicting public embarrassment alone is not enough to satisfy the fragile egos of Bosses from Hell: They always want more. They also get some satisfaction by insulting you in private, even without an audience of your peers. But the really serious harm they do is that they often enjoy punishing you further by not giving you the prime assignments you deserve—and by ridiculing you when you ask for them. Your being productive, honest, punctual, and caring enough to make useful suggestions makes them crazier; they simply ignore your abilities. The meanest—and most troubled—of them even bad-mouth you to colleagues outside the office and seem to enjoy your hurt and puzzlement when you hear about it. Some say, with false pride in their honesty, that they simply don't like you, and then challenge you to reply.

You Can Do It

I think these managers are maniacs. They're destructive and demoralize their staffs, even the workers they don't pick on. Life is too short to put up with this kind of treatment, but you have to know this is a battle you can't win by direct confrontations or by responding with the same sarcasm or abusiveness.

DEFANGING THE BOSS FROM HELL

My theory about these destructive supervisors is that the upper levels of management know about the outrageous behavior going on within their own four walls and don't do anything immediately because the work still is getting done. Or perhaps the CEO doesn't think this kind of mental torture is worthy of firing or even reprimanding the perpetrator. Perhaps the top officers don't want to set Big Bad Bosses loose on other departments. This inactivity, in my opinion, is a big mistake because of the devastating effect on employee morale.

I also think these misfits have been allowed to survive because no one has had the nerve to complain about them: Bullies often are allowed to have free rein for a long time. I don't advise individual action—it's too risky. But you can be certain that you're not the only person being mistreated. Talk to some of your fellow sufferers, keep a written log of the denigrating outbursts, and, when you have sufficient evidence to prove your point, go as a group to the human resources department or to your boss' boss and dispassionately discuss the matter. It's your only hope.

THE TYPICAL BOSS ISN'T A TYRANT

I think it's important to point out at this point that most bosses are supportive, encouraging—and very busy. Still, being

You Can Do It

Unless you're able to get enough support from your colleagues to organize collective action, handle the outbursts of your Boss from Hell with stoicism: Say nothing, do nothing. Listen quietly to the ranting and raving. Above all, don't squirm. Unfortunately, I see no advantage in trying to discuss how outrageous the boss' behavior is with your boss.

You Can Do It

Learning to deal with a wicked boss is something you can be proud of. Learning to deal with the typical, everyday boss is a necessity. If you don't learn how to shape your relationship with your supervisor, you may be forced to change jobs. And now is not the time you want to be forced to quit. Or to be fired.

human, they occasionally do lose their tempers or say something that hurts your feelings. If part of what they have to say includes constructive advice on how to improve or to correct something you did incorrectly, listen to that part and ignore the rest. Once again, being human, they'll regret having been unkind, even though what they said is true. Let it go, and things will return to normal—but immediately correct your mistake. And don't complain to your colleagues that you've been mistreated.

However, if you feel your boss ignores you or isn't supportive enough, you have to speak up. Performance reviews are a good time to do this, but you have to put a positive spin on things so it doesn't sound as if you're complaining about a perceived injustice: Explain how embarrassed you feel when you know you've let the boss down. What can you do to avoid that in the future? Don't ever accuse your boss of being unfair. Fairness has nothing to do with it. Discuss as equals what you can do to improve your performance and to avoid being reprimanded. Be informal but not casual.

GETTING ALONG WITH THE BOSS

"I have a wonderful boss but sometimes she just loses it and yells at me and everyone else," a pharmacist technician told me. "And I hate that. I asked her to have lunch with me one day—which isn't easy to do because, being my supervisor, she has to pay and I can't treat her. But she agreed to go, even

You Can Do It

Figuring out a way to get along with your boss is much more important than the boss' figuring out how to get along with you. You can be replaced. And you don't want to be.

though we are very busy." After inconsequential chitchat, the technician told his boss he had something on his mind. He wanted to do whatever he could to keep her from having so much pressure that she gets upset. What could he do? "She realized right away what I was talking about and said she had a lot of personal problems to deal with in addition to the stress at work," the technician said. "She thanked me for my support and said she would try to deal with problems in a more professional manner. She actually apologized to me! It was a good lunch. And she's kept her temper pretty much in control ever since."

STAY WHERE YOU ARE!

No matter how difficult your work situation is, no matter how much of a risk taker you are, in my opinion now is not the time to change jobs if you can avoid doing so: The job market is too unpredictable. An information technology technician was thinking about changing jobs because his job "wasn't bearable"—the standard I apply for quitting your job in a slow employment market. He said his current job is a "nightmare" because of his very insecure supervisor. He worries that his only option is to get out. He doesn't want to quit because it took him months to find the job (he even had to relocate!) after being laid off from a previous job in Silicon Valley. Unfortunately, the job he's doing is not the one he was promised, and instead of doing work he describes as "cutting-edge" (an important phrase for cyberspace professionals), he says he's stuck with routine, boring work—for which he is very well

You Can Do It

Don't even think of leaving your job, but if you have to, don't make a move before securely lining up another one.

paid. And he also knows times are tough. He wanted to know what to do. I urged him to figure out a way to hang in there, especially because he likes the company itself. He has to sit down and talk with his supervisor about the discrepancy between the job he was hired for and the one he's actually doing. Perhaps it's only temporary, to solve an urgent problem or fill an unexpected vacancy. I suggested he ask for a time frame of how long he'd be doing the work he finds so unsatisfying, and to put any promises he gets in writing. My aim was for him to try to work things out and stay on the job. I also advised him to start looking elsewhere—but not to consider leaving without another job in hand, written confirmation of employment or an employment contract, and a detailed description of the job to be filled.

REASONS NOT TO CHANGE JOBS

Most people look to their elders as role models, a practice I encourage the older I get. But right now I'm particularly impressed by Generation Xers, now in their late 20s to late 30s, who used to be known for changing jobs the moment anything unpleasant occurred. Of course, when they were just a little bit younger, there were plenty of jobs to change to and few were punished for their peripatetic ways. But according to a study conducted by a research organization based in New York City, Catalyst, and reported in *The New York Times*, Gen Xers, not previously known for their loyalty, now want to stay put and "would be happy to spend the rest of their careers with their current companies."

And just in time. I'm finding more and more people, not

just Gen Xers, who are seemingly "frozen" in place, though I would not describe them in such negative terms. In today's job market, workers no longer are looking for the fast buck of dot-com days. And that's a very smart decision because it's no longer available. A certified public accountant wrote me that she's been offered a job at a higher salary by a competitor of her present employer. It's a job fairly similar to the one she now holds—but it pays $6,000 more a year. She wants to tell her present bosses about the offer in hopes they'll match it because, she says, she really doesn't want to leave the company. I immediately warned her that reporting the offer to her present employers could be exceedingly dangerous and even cost her the job she now holds before she gets the second one. By mentioning an offer, you show you probably are job hunting, or at the very least are open to leaving. And that makes you a bad risk in the eyes of management. In most cases, revealing you have another job offer is tantamount to handing in your resignation.

Most companies will just say they are very happy for you, you ought to take the offer, and they wish you good luck and good-bye. Others might promise you the salary increase—but then let you go a few weeks later, at their convenience. I advised her if she likes her present company so much it might be wise to stay with a known quantity—and absolutely never mention the other job offer to anyone. In general, workers are far less likely to change jobs for a higher salary, according to a study of 1,800 employees by Aon Consulting. The human resources and benefits consulting firm found that 54 percent of those surveyed said they would remain with their organizations even if offered a similar job with slightly higher pay—the highest percentage since the consulting firm began its research in 1997.

THE NEW STABILITY

Though we can't control world events, many Americans are looking for stability in their jobs, at least in the aspects that they can control to some extent. And one of the few possibilities available is choosing to stay put in your job, especially if

Staying put isn't a cop-out: Not only is it harder to find a job today, it takes much longer to secure a new one. And, unfortunately, as many new hires are finding, it probably will pay less than your current one.

doing your homework indicates you're working for a company that will be around for the near future. Even top executives feel that way: According to a survey of 1,400 chief financial officers by Robert Half International, Inc., 28 percent ranked stability as the most important consideration in employment. Stability was number one, over other factors such as salary level, career advancement, corporate culture, and stock options. I didn't do the research, but I'll bet stability wasn't even mentioned a decade ago.

MORE REASONS NOT TO CHANGE JOBS

If you work in an industry that is declining or disappearing overseas, such as manufacturing, then you probably should be contemplating not just a job change but also a career change. Even in that event, don't move too quickly. Check out every possibility in advance and make sure the industry you switch to is a flourishing one. For everyone else, however, this might be the time to sit tight and see what happens to the economy, particularly if you are the primary support of your family.

A major reason to keep your present job is health benefits. You don't want to lose them. In good times, I am always the first to complain that the need for health benefits for themselves or family members often keeps workers trapped in jobs they hate. I still believe that health-care insurance needs to be delivered in a different way, one that has nothing to do with whether you have a job that offers them. Yet now I'm saying that they are a very good reason to keep your present job.

Even at a time when jobs are scarce, people still have dreams of new jobs, new locations, and new businesses, even of better mousetraps. Now is the time to plan how to make those dreams become a reality—and you'll be ready to go when the economy improves.

Grim economic forecasts are another reason to remain "frozen." At the same time that worker productivity is up—smart employees are giving their jobs their all—there is less lucrative overtime and many companies are cutting workers back to less than 40 hours a week. "I've been making good money when you count in the overtime," a plant worker told me. "But my dream is to make a geographical move to a larger city. I know that involves my leaving my present job without having another one. And I've also heard that most of the plants are giving workers overtime, as they are here. Even though I'm single, I'm worried about giving up my security. What's your advice?" It's only because I'm a pragmatist—not a Killer of the Dream—that I told the factory worker that these are not good economic times and most people would be wise to hold on to the jobs they have, especially workers in manufacturing, at least until things shake out. Jobs in manufacturing, I added, are pretty tight right now, and most plants have plenty of local applicants. But I advised him if he does want to take the risk to make sure he has saved up at least six months of living expenses.

RETENTION IS AN EMPLOYER'S ISSUE, TOO

Because of the high cost of turnover, employee retention—making you want to stay on the job—concerns employers, too. Even with a plethora of job applicants, management still is wise enough to create work environments that are supportive

You Can Do It

Staying in your present job doesn't mean you have to put your career on hold. Being focused on what you're currently doing will still allow you to move ahead and advance your career. In the next chapter, I'll show you how to do just that.

and encouraging. They still want to reward you for work well done and to make sure you have a challenging and satisfying job. Work/life benefits (see Chapter 7) still are a top priority at major companies, where, even though recruitment is no longer a problem, hanging on to the best employees is a goal that has to be met both for the bottom line and for productivity. I want to emphasize that employers don't want to fire you, don't want you to move on, and don't want you to change careers. They, too, crave stability. Hopefully, this knowledge will give you the courage to stay in a job that in more prosperous times you would quickly leave. And you can still do that when the cycle of job scarcity swings to job plenitude.

chapter 5

ADVANCING YOUR CAREER

The road to success in today's job market has changed considerably. The first part of the trip involves simply keeping the job you now have (see Chapter 4). The second part is to position yourself to move forward in tiny increments, even baby steps, to reach your goal.

It's no longer possible to start in the middle and quickly rocket to the top of your profession, accompanied by flashing lights and roaring engines. Instead, you probably will have to start your career acceleration somewhere near the bottom. Slow and steady, with no sharp turns, is the road map when jobs are scarce. Companies are very slow to make decisions—particularly about promotions, but also about any moves, even sideways, that usually are accompanied by pay or expense increases.

Your career will not move forward, even slowly, by itself. You will have to be both the navigator and the driver in order to propel it, if not to the stratosphere or even Cloud 9, at least to the next level. Be proactive in directing your career. No one else can do it for you.

EMPLOYERS STILL NEED EMPLOYEES

Despite the fierce competition for jobs and promotions and the ever-present specter of layoffs, downsizings, and bankruptcies, there is something positive working strongly in your favor. Employers still need employees. Someone has to do the job. That's why workers are the strongest assets a business has—and deep down, no matter how cavalier some employers are during times when jobs are scarce, they don't want you to leave. Regardless of how often you might be told that you can be easily replaced, it still takes time and money to do so.

A recent study of 500 executives by InsightExpress, an online market research firm, shows that 59 percent of the top suits report they're worried that recent layoffs will induce their remaining employees—the ones they kept because they are productive—to look for new jobs. "While employers have the upper hand in the job market today, they still need to pay attention to employee concerns," said Lee Smith, chief operating officer of the company. "When a key employee leaves, so do customers—and that's money out the door."

THE SILVER LINING

The fact that employers realize they need productive employees at every level plays to your benefit in another way. Smart and informed managers have to do the most with the employees they have left after drastic layoffs and reductions of staff. Since you're still there, now is your chance to be noticed, acknowledged, trained, and moved ahead—not only because

Companies want to keep quality people, and one way they do that is to give them promotions. Be a quality employee. Now is the time to hunker down.

Your company's downsizing, as sad as it is to see it happen, can be your "upsizing." But even though there is a silver lining, nothing will be given to you on a silver platter. You will have to work hard at moving ahead.

you're qualified but because the exodus of so many of your colleagues has opened doors for you to advance.

The gridlock is gone. You have the competitive edge because you're on the inside and because employers are starting to promote from within rather than searching for new talent outside their corporate walls, which was the way many companies filled openings in the good old economic days. "I never thought I'd have a chance to move ahead," an advertising copywriter told me. "In fact, I was worried about keeping the job I had. But we let 10 people go in my department—that's 50 percent of our staff—and the rest of us had to pick up the slack. I worked my butt off to make sure all the work got done and to continue to meet our production goals. And, to my surprise, I was finally given the promotion and title I've wanted for the past three years. I only got a very small raise but I'm not complaining. Not at all."

DEFENSIVE ACTION

As a survivor of today's workplace, your number one challenge is to make sure your name is not on the next list of layoffs or even buyouts (although buyouts are better because you usually get a better financial deal as you exit). To avoid the executioner, take time to develop a personal strategy for your professional future. Unfortunately, the best approach to it in today's chaotic times is a negative albeit realistic one: Keep in mind that you may be just one heartbeat away from being downsized. You can't afford to feel safe, even while you're planning the steps necessary to advance your career.

On the positive side, you are in a good spot because you represent some prime advantages to your employer:

- You're already on the inside.

- You've been on the job for at least a few years.

- You are completely aware of the company culture, how to get things done, and what direction your industry is heading in.

But having these assets doesn't mean you can relax. You still have to have a plan.

A ONE-YEAR PLAN

The traditional work plan has always been five years, plotting exactly where you want to be in that time frame. For years I've been saying, half in jest, that my five-year plan is to get through tomorrow. And, considering the volatility of today's job market, a five-year plan is somewhat naive. I advise a one-year plan—and if you want to go beyond that, do it separately.

The starting point is to consider what constitutes career advancement for you. Is it:

- A new title?

- Expanded responsibilities?

- Making a lateral move to a different department?

- Getting additional training or even an advanced degree?

And then ask yourself how much time you want to devote to the enormous effort of moving ahead.

After you give these questions serious thought and come up with answers that work for you, design your one-year plan. Also include in the plan these important factors:

Being average won't get you where you want to go. You have to be superior. Every day.

- What you will have to do to get more responsibilities and more important assignments?

- How to do your present job in an exemplary fashion.

- How to get additional training.

- How to stay abreast of developments in your profession.

- How to get noticed by your managers.

All in the next 12 months.

IN THE BEGINNING

Plotting your future serves one of the same purposes as that of keeping your resume current: It helps you to pay daily attention to your job and to face the reality of what is possible and what isn't. Today a career plan of any length isn't to create a path to your dream job; it's how to move up a few rungs of the career ladder in your present job. Your next step in creating your one-year plan is to sit down and do it. If you've thought it out carefully, it should only take you an hour.

Put everything in writing or in your computer (at home, not at work). Update it as your circumstances or your goals change.

- What is the next promotion you have your eye on?

- What does the job require?

- What skills do you already have that qualify you for that important next step?

You Can Do It

A plan is just that: a plan. It is not an amendment to the U.S. Constitution. Don't feel defeated if you're unable to do every part of it. Be elated about whatever you manage to achieve. Look at your career plan, even with limited goals, as a guidepost to follow as closely as you can, at least until the economy is on a more even keel.

- What skills do you need that you don't have?
- Which manager is responsible for filling the position when it opens up?
- Do you already have a relationship with this person?
- Who in the company will help you achieve your next step?
- Who will be your mentor?
- What salary do you think you should be earning by next year? (Caution: Remember, in a slow economy with frozen or very low monetary wage increases, salary can't be the only test of your achievements—or you may feel as if you're failing when you're really not.)

How to Make Being There Work for You

If you're highly motivated—and you will have to be in order to get to the next step of your career—your personal strategy, the one you delineated in your one-year plan, should include the following:

- Finding a role model and/or a mentor.
- Networking internally.

Don't make a nuisance of yourself, but try to be there when needed. And don't be shy about asking questions about how to do your job better. Then, do your job better.

- Being a good team player.

- Overcoming or learning to live with obstacles in your way.

Visibility is another asset. Managers promote the people they're aware of, whom they talk to on a daily basis, and whom they come to depend on. Those are the people who also get the best assignments and the promotions.

THE OLD RULES OF CAREER ADVANCEMENT

In the early 1980s, when I was made Jobs editor of *The Chicago Tribune*, my columns advised ambitious workers to be well organized; to build solid relationships with their colleagues and managers; to be flexible and eager to help, even with tasks not in their job descriptions; to be well-informed about the strategic direction the company is taking—and above all, to roll up their sleeves and pitch in at all times. My advice hasn't changed over the years. The old rules still apply.

Make yourself indispensable. Do more than what's expected of you. Get broad-based experience right in your own department. Whatever works is good. Very good.

But they now have an added urgency. I have always written from the perspective of the job seeker or employee. I've always been on their "side." I have never wanted anyone to work unusually long hours or to do extra work without compensation for it. An unusually crowded labor market, however, calls for exceptional accomplishments to make yourself the most valuable employee in the company—and to make sure you are successful.

ROLE MODELS

Having role models is something most people talk about but never take seriously. But you should. Someone who has succeeded in achieving the goals you have in mind is worth observing closely and emulating—not necessarily imitating but seeing what it actually takes to get to where you want to go. You don't have to know your role models personally. You can watch them from afar. Close-up is better, of course, but that's not always possible. And they don't even have to be alive to inspire you. Trace their steps. Analyze what they've done, when they did it, and what worked or didn't work for them.

Many ambitious business students tell me they want to be like Jack Welch, former head of General Electric. Students in the "caring" professions want to emulate Martin Luther King Jr., Nelson Mandela, and Florence Nightingale. Artists study Pablo Picasso, Rosa Bonheur, and Salvador Dali. Athletes worship Michael Jordan and his achievements. Future entertainers follow every performer ever mentioned in *People* magazine. Journalists still want to be like Bob Woodward (or is it Robert Redford?) and Carl Bernstein (or is it Dustin Hoffman?) of *All the President's Men* movie fame. As for me, my role models long have been Gloria Steinem and Mike Royko, an unlikely coupling except that both are exceptional journalists. As a longtime contributor to *Ms.* magazine, I've been lucky enough to have Gloria Steinem's direct and personal encouragement over the years. And the late Mike Royko, my *The Chicago Tribune* with whom I used to play tennis, did me the honor of giving me one of his special names (remember Governor Moonbeam, his name for former

You can pick anyone you want to be your role model. The person never even has to know of your admiration.

California Governor Jerry Brown?). Royko called me Ms. LibLob, and since it came from one of my role models, I try very hard to live up to it.

HAVING A MENTOR

A mentor is much more close-up and personal than a role model and plays a much more direct role in your career advancement. A mentor is someone you know personally who understands the ins and outs of your industry, profession, and job—and who is willing to nurture and help you advance in your career. Having a mentor, particularly if the mentor is a higher-up at your present place of employment, is so essential to moving ahead that career experts often jokingly suggest if you can't find someone agreeable to helping you on a voluntary basis, hire a mentor. Of course you can't do that, so here's how to find a mentor, someone you can go to freely for advice and who has time to give you inside tips and information.

- Look around at your own department to ascertain who might be amenable to teaching you the ropes.

- If no one is available, look throughout the company for people in a position similar to the one you're working toward.

- If no one in your company wants to mentor you, seek out professionals in your industry at other companies.

If no one person is available to mentor you, ask several people, each an expert in one area in which you need some input, to give you guidance in their specialties. Explain up front you will need only a few minutes of their time each week. It shouldn't take more than that to glean the information you need on a regular basis.

- Make contact with Super Achievers in your professional or personal networks and ask one to be your mentor.

- If all else fails, try to establish a relationship with someone on the Internet who can give you helpful direction. And while you're seeking a mentor of your own, offer to help mentor others.

NETWORK, NETWORK, NETWORK

I strongly believe in networking because it's an effective way to advance your career. A network, according to the second definition in *Webster's New World Dictionary*, is "a system of interconnected or cooperating individuals." That description of the exchange of helpful information explains why networks, both formal and informal, continue to grow and function effectively for all members. But I also like the first definition in the dictionary, which is somewhat esoteric but also delineates the exact process of networking: "Any arrangement of fabric or parallel wires, threads, etc., crossed at regular intervals by others fastened to them so as to leave open spaces." Networks can be made up of informal groupings of three or more people who want to advance their careers and are willing to help you do the same. Sometimes, they're called friends.

Be selective about what networks you join or form. Don't spread yourself too thin. Target your networking to meet your present needs. And remember networking isn't all work: It's actually a fun way to meet people in your own field.

Other informal groups, formed at work, are called in-house networks and are made up of colleagues with the same interests and the ability to share information. More formal groupings are professional associations, composed of people in the same field or of people across many disciplines but with the same interests. I've been a member of The Chicago Network since its founding in 1979. I always describe this successful network as being made up of 199 highly successful, outstanding Chicago women—and me. The Chicago Network always has been an invaluable source of information and of experts to interview for my newspaper columns. One of the members, for instance, is Ann Marie Lipinski, first woman editor-in-chief of *The Chicago Tribune*—and my boss!

ATTENDING NETWORKING MEETINGS

Although the network directory with names, titles, addresses (including e-mail), and phone numbers is a handbook of connections you can put to good use, attending networking meetings can directly help you quickly outpace your one-year plan of job advancement. Meet as many of the members as you can and ask for their cards. Make contacts and stay in touch with them. Stand up at the meetings and ask for whatever it is you need professionally: That's what a business network is for. Volunteer for network committees. Contribute to its newsletter. Take as guests to network meetings people you want to get to know better: They'll appreciate the contacts, too. Let members of the network know about anything good that happens to

You Can Do It

Networking isn't only about taking; it's also about giving. Remember those interconnected links. When you have some inside or helpful information, share it with friends or colleagues who need it. They'll do the same. It's called not only networking but also synergy.

you, such as a special assignment or a promotion—and also about some of your problems. They can help you.

BEING A GOOD TEAM PLAYER

Before you are hired, managers want to know if you can do the job. After you're on the job, they want to know if you're cooperative and work well with other people. Since so many projects now are assigned to teams rather than individuals, whether or not you're a team player is a factor carefully scrutinized by employers and may decide your future in your present job. "Virtually all business work is accomplished through other people," write James Waldroop and Timothy Butler in their book, *The 12 Bad Habits That Hold Good People Back* (Doubleday). "Having the right knowledge and the will to succeed are not enough." The authors suggest "stepping outside of your own skin" to understand someone else's point of view. Teamwork is a collective effort, only as effective as the sum of its parts: You have to understand and be supportive of your team members or you won't be able to work together.

Teamwork, at most companies worldwide, still makes the best work. And you want to be the best. Understand the role each team member plays; be aware of who has which assignment and when it has to be done. Give your input to each project but listen just as carefully as you want to be listened to when others give you advice. Work closely with the members. Don't show up at the end with your share of the work completed. You need to communicate. Help others and they'll help you. Iron out any problems as quickly as possible so the work isn't stalled. Be friendly and accommodating at all times. Be a good team player and soon you will be team leader.

OBSTACLES IN YOUR WAY

Everyone who is qualified should be able to advance as rapidly as their talents permit them to. But the upward climb, particularly in a corporation, isn't always that easy. I get phone calls almost every day from people who say they were passed over for promotion even though they were the most qualified. Unless they were rejected for discriminatory reasons and want to file a lawsuit, there's nothing they can do about the missed opportunity. Women and minorities are the groups most ignored when it comes to moving ahead or moving to the very top.

With only a very few exceptions, the nation's top companies are run by white men who tend to promote the people who look like them, act like them, worked with them, went to the same schools as they did—and who play golf. Minorities and women are ignored at staff meetings, which are dominated by men. "I'm the only woman and I always am made to feel as if I'm invisible, even though I've worked so hard to be ranked high enough to attend these important meetings," said a woman executive who is Hispanic. "And if I am able to get a word in, no one listens. I even find out later that someone else has taken credit for my ideas." What she is experiencing is called the glass ceiling, an effective barrier that keeps women from moving ahead no matter how qualified they are or how hard they work.

Minority men suffer from the same syndrome. Discrimination is an effective roadblock, so you will have to fight it in whatever way you can. Legal action is one way, after creating a paper trail of the discriminatory incidents. But most people want a job, not a lawsuit, so they have to do extra work to overcome this offensive obstacle. To overcome the negative perceptions that are so unfair and not based in fact but in ignorance, keep a detailed record of what you do and say and make sure the right people see it. Get credit for your accomplishments.

Sexual harassment is another obstacle women face in trying to move ahead. Men who harass on the surface are making unwelcome sexual overtures, but at the same time they're also effectively keeping women out of certain jobs. Sexual harassment, like other forms of discrimination, is illegal. It has to be reported. It has to be stopped. Most large companies, burned by expensive lawsuits, will not condone this behavior. You shouldn't, either. Speak up. As employment lawyer Sheribel Rothenberg observes, "If we don't speak up, what will we tell our daughters?"

OTHER ANNOYANCES

Other annoyances can become obstacles if you let them get to you. Bothersome coworkers, unsympathetic bosses, unrealistic deadlines, too much work, difficult working conditions such as lack of privacy, company surveillance of everything you do, lack of respect—any one of these things can drive even the most even-tempered person up the office wall. In tough economic times, you have to roll with the punches.

That doesn't mean you should quietly take any form of abuse. It does mean you must keep control of your emotions and try to solve each problem in a professional and dignified way. Try to put each obstacle in its proper perspective: Will it cost you your job? Will it cost you your sanity? It may be some comfort to know you're not alone; your colleagues are going

As consummate professional Jo Ann Nathan, a landscape historian, suggests, rearrange your "landscape" when you feel frustrated. Nathan's advice is to "concentrate on the product. Forget the sideshow." And one of her favorite adages also is to the point: "Keep your eye on the doughnut, not the hole!"

through the same things you are. While trying to deal with the obstacles, also keep in mind that overall you like your job fairly well, want to keep it, and want to advance in it.

SOME CHANCES TO SHINE

What's wonderful about the world of work is that you are given plenty of opportunities, or can create them, to shine, to present yourself in a good light. The ones that are most commonplace—and therefore underestimated as important vehicles to show your stuff—are job postings, performance reviews, salary reviews, cross training, staff meetings, volunteer work, building your reputation, and, the very best one of all, when you're promoted.

Job Postings

When job openings are announced in an open forum, everyone has a chance to try for them, not just those on the A list. That's why I am such an enthusiast about job postings—they're such an equal opportunity. Internal job listings provide real chances to advance your career: If you're qualified for the job, first talk to your supervisor about your plans. Then, apply by listing your credentials and accomplishments. If you're turned down for the job, find out why and make sure you are given whatever training will qualify you for the next opening. But even if you don't get the job—or if you really don't want it—use the posting as a chance to show you are an active player, that you want to move ahead. Once again, ask for the necessary training to improve your skills. You'll soon come to the attention of management as a go-getter, plus you'll also know what the next job up entails. No wonder I love cross-departmental, inter-divisional job postings!

Performance Appraisals

The tricky part about these annual reviews is that they're not supposed to be connected with your salary review—but they are, of course. Officially, a performance review is an evaluation by your manager of the work you have done. Prepare for it as you would for a job interview, because it is very similar. This is your chance to market yourself vigorously to the one person who matters most in your career: your boss.

Bring with you to the review your list of accomplishments and be prepared to show how they match your job description. You are the one who should emphasize your strengths. Your manager will point out your weaknesses. Greet both with the same reaction, because you want to improve even more. Ask what you can do and what training is available. Be completely honest and forthcoming in these reviews. The information you get is extremely critical in advancing your career. Feel free to mention work-related activities that you feel should enhance your value to the company: helping people in other departments, representing your company at community affairs, mentoring other employees, or organizing social events for your colleagues that give a boost to morale. Above all, stress your teamwork skills.

Teamwork is the buzzword in today's performance reviews. Ask your supervisor what your goals should be for the following year and be explicit about what you think they should be. Listen attentively to what your manager says because the boss also has prepared for this session and knows exactly what your level of performance needs to be. Ask for specific examples if your boss says you have certain weaknesses. Also ask for examples of things management thinks you do well. You can also mention what salary you think you should be earning by the next performance review, even though salary is supposed to be taboo in these discussions.

Though traditionally it is your manager and only your manager whose opinions make up your final assessment, many employers have instituted the 360-degree form of evaluations. It's a "full circle" of appraisal and involves not just your boss but also other people you deal with, such as colleagues, team members, subordinates, and even clients. At some companies, you are allowed to pick some of the people you want to participate in your appraisal. The 360-degree appraisal is a good idea, I think, because then you're not at the mercy of the manager's opinion only. And because I'm always on the side of employees, I think it's perfectly okay to stack the deck in your favor.

But that's why 360-degree reviews have full credibility only when the other participants just give opinions and are not asked to give you a numerical rating. Even with 360-degree performance reviews, it is your manager who has the final say—and the responsibility for the work you do. However, you need to keep in mind that you have to make the review work for you.

Salary Reviews

Just as performance reviews are not supposed to be salary reviews, salary reviews aren't supposed to be performance reviews, but no two factors could be more closely linked. However, there is a major difference in their execution. While there is a bit of leverage in influencing your final performance evaluation, there is very little in salary reviews. The amount of increase—if any—probably was budgeted last year, and there is nothing you can do to change it. What you will be negotiating for is a better increase next year. Because of economic uncertainty, many firms—those that haven't instituted salary freezes or percentage annual pay cuts—are sticking with their initial plans, made when times were better, to keep merit increases at somewhere just under 4 percent. But almost half of the largest firms won't be giving bonuses for a while.

Despite these negatives, you still have to sell yourself to your manager, showing your added value to the company and proving that you earn your salary. If you feel you're making less than your colleagues doing the same work, point out how you would like to be brought up to equity in the near future. But don't look sullen or unhappy; these are uncertain economic times. That's why I also don't think now is the time to ask for more vacation days, free parking, country club membership, or other perks. In times like these, your job is your perk.

More Education and Cross Training

If your boss has pointed out to you that you need certain skills shored up, ask what courses you should take and whether you can learn them in-house or by attending colleges. Perhaps you need an advanced degree or certification (see Chapter 6). Ask how additional learning will help your career. Ask about the possibility of cross training—working in another job in your own department or in another department for a few months—to learn skills that you lack and that will help your own department's productivity. Because you will learn how to do other people's jobs, you should point out that you will be able to fill in or take over during absences. It will also help you advance your career. Take whatever classes you can, even if you have to pay for them yourself. A clerk in an insurance office was asked by her supervisor to take additional responsibilities. She asked me what to do because no additional salary was offered. She liked being asked but she didn't like working without full compensation for her efforts. I agreed with her that it's very nice to be paid for what you do, but not to pass up such a wonderful opportunity to move ahead. I told her to take on the extra work, do it very well, and then ask about more money, a higher grade, and perhaps a higher title. Taking on the work would pay off, I promised her. And within only a few months, it did.

Being Visible

One of the easiest ways to market yourself so that you're the one chosen for the next promotion that comes up is to be a familiar figure. Being a good communicator, which means both speaking well and listening carefully, will get you the respect you deserve. Voice your opinions at small gatherings, at staff meetings, and especially when your boss asks you what you think about a new project. Be a known quantity, not a mystery worker.

Volunteer for special projects and company-wide task forces. You'll work with people you've never worked with before and they'll be able to attest to your professionalism—and you to theirs. Make sure you're a player in these projects, not an observer. Do volunteer work in your community at an agency you really want to help—and then make your manager aware of what you're doing outside the company that brings it more prestige and customers.

When you do something you think is noteworthy, make

sure it's noted. Write down the information and send it to your company newsletter; no one can do that but you. Remember, you're not the only one doing it. Each of your competitors is. Be aware of your reputation, because it can make or break your career. How do other people perceive your character? Is your reputation what you want it to be? Do you communicate your personal standards in a professional way? Your integrity is the most important constant in your daily life. Hold it close to your heart because your reputation depends on it. And a good reputation opens doors; a bad one slams them shut.

Getting Promoted

When you do get the promotion you so richly deserve, don't sit back all alone on your laurels. Try to include as many others as you can in your success. Thank your manager for believing in you. Thank your colleagues and team members for making you look good. Tell your mentor immediately. Contact and thank your networking buddies at the same time that you share your excitement. Above all, don't burn any bridges. A sales manager was promoted recently, much to his surprise. "I didn't know I was in such good graces," he said, "but I had worked very hard and very well and it was wonderful getting the recognition I feel I deserved." Euphoric as he was about his new post, he didn't forget the people who helped him get there. One of the first things he did was to get his former assistant promoted, too. And the second thing he did was find out every detail of his new assignment so that he could prove his bosses were right to have enough belief in him to move him ahead.

Do everything you can to advance your career, but take the time to put all of your accomplishments in writing. You will be surprised how often you pull that list out and use it to prove your worth.

BEING SUCCESSFUL

Positioning yourself for success is a strategic move that will not only help you move ahead but will also help ensure your present job. Because you do your job well, get along with your teammates, respect your colleagues, understand the direction of the company, have upgraded skills, are active in the community, volunteer for any and all projects, apply for jobs that are posted, and more—all these things are to your credit. You deserve to be promoted. You're a hard worker and know what you're doing. Each of these activities is straightforward, honest, and direct. But sometimes it also takes a bit of subterfuge and subtlety to get to where you deserve to go.

SCHMOOZING HELPS

I hate the words: schmoozing, apple-polishing, buttering up, brownnosing, sucking up—and worse. But there's one thing about schmoozing, if it's done quietly and inoffensively. It works. Being nice to the people who can help you isn't such a terrible thing to do. Advocates of apple-polishing think what it really is, it seems, is "building bridges." The fact is that workers who are liked by their supervisors and colleagues are more successful. A small percentage of them, to their credit, are liked because they're likable and don't have to do too much schmoozing to get recognition.

You Can Do It

If you closely follow the suggestions in this chapter, you'll be able to take advantage of whatever opportunities arise. But to make absolutely certain you are positioned to achieve your career goals and to be in line for the promotions you want, continue your professional training and education. It's your ticket to even further success. (See Chapter 6.)

Everybody else has to reach out in some way to the people they come in contact with, not only in their own department but in other areas of the company. And that reach should extend to being on a name-recognition basis with the CEO and other top officers, no matter how rarely you come in contact with them. A polished apple-polisher myself, I like to describe buttering up others as another way you can network and expand your personal contacts, particularly with people in the company you don't usually do business with. It's one of the things you can do to be successful, and when you are, be aware that people now are schmoozing with you.

chapter 6

IT'S EDUCATION, EDUCATION, AND EDUCATION

ontinuing—and continuous—education is your investment in your present job and in the future of your career. Besides, lifelong learning is something no one can ever take away from you, no matter whether the economy is dramatically rising upward or just as dramatically sinking lower. It's yours to keep forever.

Adding to your skills is job protection, and knowledge gives you the power to get a job, keep it, and advance in your career. And learning, even for learning's sake alone, stimulates your mind. According to educators, in down times like these more and more people take additional courses, sign up for or ask to be included in on-site training at their places of employment, complete unfinished high school or college degrees, and work toward certification in their professional fields.

You Can Do It

Why are more workers pursuing more training and education? Because they're smart. And they're going to be even smarter.

EDUCATION MEANS A GOOD JOB

The U.S. Bureau of Labor Statistics (BLS)—that wonderful source of information and edifying insights for U.S. workers—reports that job categories that generally require an associate degree or more education are projected to grow faster than the 14 percent average for all occupations. In contrast, all other categories are expected to grow less than 14 percent. Additionally, occupations requiring postsecondary vocational degrees or academic degrees, which accounted for 20 percent of all jobs in 2000, will account for 42 percent of total job growth from 2000 to 2010, asserts Daniel E. Hecker, an economist at the BLS. And *Training & Development* magazine puts it this way: "Ideas are the currency of the future. They break down barriers, create opportunities, and enrich lives."

THE CASE FOR EDUCATION

The continuing demand for education by employers and the information age we live in is shown in changes in employment relative to education, according to a report of the Employment Policy Foundation. The study, which I consider significant for our times, shows that from September 2000 to October 2001 (a period of time that included 9/11), more than 1.2 million new jobs went to applicants with postsecondary training—in other words, more than a high school diploma. But job loss—more than 1.9 million jobs—was concentrated among workers who did not have even a high school diploma.

And what effect did September 11 have on educational requirements by employers? The foundation's study concludes that "the employment impact of the September 11 attacks has

Mint your own "currency" by getting all the education and new skills that you can.

You Can Do It

Though many employers continue to lay off and downsize in order to stay in business (see Chapter 1), other industries such as security, pharmaceuticals, defense, and health care have a different challenge. They can't find qualified people to fill their job openings. And the mismatch is costly to both the potential employer and the unsuccessful job seeker.

magnified the importance of skills and education." Job growth for vocational school graduates and those with bachelor's degrees continued strong in the aftermath. "Job losses were concentrated among those with the least education."

MORE EDUCATION, MORE TRAINING

Occupations with the most job growth projected by the U.S. Department of Labor are the very ones that require the most skills, the most lifelong learning. One exception, however, is the job of federalized airport security workers, who will not have to have even a high school diploma. Though they will have "intensive" testing, according to the government, they won't need that diploma. The shock and outrage expressed by congressional leaders and even average Americans at this announcement show how strongly the nation believes in having at least a high school diploma. And some of that shock and outrage should also have come from the security workers themselves, who have a very challenging and demanding job! But qualifying to be an airport security worker is an exception to the prevailing rule that education and training are essential.

Take a look at some jobs and what their bottom-line requirements are, once again according to the BLS. Compare the educational requirements for the best jobs to the requirements for jobs that very often are dead-end ones—such as airport security personnel.

You Can Do It

Every day in every way, we grow bigger, better, smarter, and more secure by soaking up every bit of knowledge we can, particularly about our jobs.

At least a bachelor's degree. Systems analysts, managers and executives, computer engineers, elementary and secondary school teachers, university professors, and computer programmers.

On-the-job training. Retail salespeople, cashiers, home health aides, janitors and housekeepers, receptionists, waiters, airport security guards, fast-food workers, child care workers, groundskeepers, packagers, clerks, and correctional officers.

Work experience. Office and administrative support staff, factory supervisors, and assembly line workers.

While it's my strong belief that all labor is honorable, if you want to advance your career, which category would you prefer to be in?

THE MONEY CONNECTION

More education means more money in a job market that places a premium on education and skills. The Employment Policy Foundation report observes that more and more positions are being created in the technical, professional, and management occupations, each of which requires ongoing improvement of skills and constant updating of information. And if you meet those requirements, you probably will be able to get the salary you deserve.

Basing its data on the Bureau of Labor Statistics' ongoing Current Population Survey of earnings and education, here's what the foundation found (shown in Table 6.1).

Table 6.1 Earnings and Education

Education	Average Weekly Earnings	Average Annual Earnings	Lifetime Earnings
No high school diploma	$410	$21,314	$852,577
High school diploma	$588	$30,560	$1,222,396
Two-year vocational degree	$708	$36,833	$1,473,335
Two-year college or associate degree	$733	$38,118	$1,524,703
Bachelor's degree	$949	$49,344	$1,973,760
Master's degree	$1,109	$57,676	$2,307,025
Professional or doctorate degree	$1,376	$71,573	$2,862,914

Source: Employment Policy Foundation; Bureau of Labor Statistics, U.S. Department of Labor.

You Can Do It

You don't have to be a rocket scientist with a Ph.D. (but if you are you probably will earn more than $2 million more over a lifetime than someone without a high school diploma) to figure out that having the necessary education credentials means having a lot of extra money in your pocket.

THAT BACHELOR'S DEGREE

Since a bachelor's degree is the academic credential most Americans seek (it has actually replaced the high school diploma as the bottom-line educational requirement in an increasing number of jobs), it's encouraging to note that the highest-paying occupations usually require at least a bachelor's degree. The *Occupational Outlook Quarterly*, a publication of the hardworking Bureau of Labor Statistics, studied annual earnings in 1998 for certain highly desirable jobs. Table 6.2 lists the

Table 6.2   Selected Salaries for Jobs Requiring College Degrees

Job	Salary
Advertising and sales managers	$57,300
Materials engineers	$57,970
Lawyers	$78,170
Aircraft pilots and flight engineers	$91,700
Dentists	$110,160
Physicians	$124,820

Source: Occupational Outlook Quarterly, Bureau of Labor Statistics. U.S. Department of Labor.

You Can Do It

Why earn less when you can earn more simply by having the right educational background—and the powerful leverage of continuing education?

annual salaries they came up with for those who had the entry requirements of a college degree.

CONQUERING CYBERSPACE

You hear the expressions "knowledge worker" and "computer literacy" a lot these days. What they both mean is that information is essential in today's technological society, and the way to get it and transmit it—and increasingly in order to do your job—is to be a skilled computer user. No one is born knowing how to use a computer or its multitude of programs, even the little kids you see who are so comfortable at the keyboard. Everything is learned, one of the few things the new technology hasn't changed.

You Can Do It

To keep up with the demands of today's job world, you have to be completely at ease at your computer. And if you're not, it's a signal you absolutely need more training and guidance in how to make cyberspace work for you.

THE COMPUTER CONNECTION

If you're not already linked up with everyone else in your office or plant, you will be. If you're a telecommuter (see Chapter 7), you will have to be, out of necessity to get your work done and to communicate with your colleagues. As more and more jobs are automated, your skills and abilities in this high-tech society will be more critical. No one expects you to be able to set up a network computer system (unless that's your job), to design new programs (though what a plus that would be for your manager!), nor to know every single sound byte of the World Wide Web. But you are expected to be able to sit down and do your work at your computer without weeks of training and to be your own personal information manager.

Computer use involves reasoning, and reasoning is the reason that personal computer on your desk at work will make such a dramatic and positive difference in your career progress—far beyond the immediacy and wonder of worldwide e-mail at your fingertips! No matter what we label our economic trends (information collection and distribution) or our electronic progress (the technological age), the new frontier of the twenty-first century, in both turbulent and calm labor markets, is the brain, the organ you use to learn and grow and advance your career. Keeping your brain alert, stretching and using it, especially in the area of computers and computer programs, is your very own Save key: It will save your job.

You Can Do It

Sign up for every computer course your employer offers. Learn all you can about every program you use to do your job. Request from your employer additional training outside the workplace to brush up on your computer skills—and ask for it by e-mail, using all the bells and whistles you can to show how much you are at home at the keyboard. And if your employer hasn't anything to offer you, look at the end of this chapter for a list of web sites with information about courses you can access from the Internet.

The service-producing sector, which also was hit hard by the turmoil of 9/11, still is the area producing the most jobs, and almost all of those jobs require people who are computer literate. Often, the term "computer literacy," when employed by your employer, encompasses other skills the work requires, such as being adaptable to new hardware and software, being able to work on your computer in a large, noisy office or the (hopefully) quiet of your home. It means being able to communicate instantly with your clients, customers, colleagues, and managers. It means being flexible and patient. But its basic meaning is knowledge, knowledge of the ins and outs of cyberspace. "Computer Literacy" covers a lot of sins. Make sure you're a major "sinner."

LIFELONG LEARNING

The U.S. Department of Labor has estimated that three out of every four workers now employed will need retraining for the new jobs that are created daily by new technology. Not only are thousands of workers studying on their own time to improve their skills, but employers worldwide, who don't have a nanosecond to waste, also are spending money and time every year to bring their employees up-to-date on everything from those all-important computers to communication skills, customer service, marketing, problem solving, teamwork, and much, much more.

Training is so important that, according to the American Society for Training and Development, companies have been spending an estimated $65 billion a year on employee training—at least that was the size of their budget before the current economic turndown. My point is that the need for training doesn't disappear in a recession; in fact, it accelerates because it is vital for companies to get the most out of the employees that remain on staff. That's why all the large employers devote entire departments to worker training. Some even have their own "colleges"—actual campuses at which their workers study and learn. Others invite accredited institutions to come in and teach various courses, including foreign languages, and to offer degree programs, including bachelor's and

You Can Do It

Improve your intellectual capabilities by reading books or viewing videos in your area of expertise, taking general courses, enrolling in a degree program, attending lectures and conferences, enrolling in seminars—and whenever you can, get your company not only to pay for these programs (which they can deduct from their income tax) but also to allow you to attend them, if necessary, during working hours. The company won't just be doing you a favor; it will in turn be the beneficiary of your studies. But in times when raises are so scarce and so many salaries are frozen, reimbursing your expenses or giving you time off for classes is something your boss can do in lieu of a raise, and the company gets a tax deduction.

master's degrees. Smart employers know that training and being up-to-date keep them competitive. The Radisson Hotels & Resorts, based in Minneapolis, announced in 2002—after the recession began and after the terrorists attacks—that it was instituting "training enhancements" for its corporate and hotel employees to access training and education both in person and online. And why did Radisson, which has more than 430 locations in 60 countries, decide to do this in the face of hard times for the hospitality industry? "We want to help our brand become best in class," said Jay Witzel, president and chief operating officer.

And the classroom is the best place to do that.

Still, it is up to you to research, direct, and make provisions for your own continuing education program.

Spreading the Word

You yourself might want to be the one who spreads the word that workplace education should be a value embraced by all employers, just as lifelong learning should be a personal goal of every worker. "I recently was laid off from my factory job," an assembly line manager told me. "I knew it was coming so I took every training course I could—even though I had only a high school diploma, and that was from 30 years ago! It wasn't easy working hard all day and going to school at night and weekends to get my associate degree in management—I found I really liked managing—and learn additional computer skills since our plant was almost completely computerized. But I knew I was investing in my future and the company was paying most of my bills."

You Can Do It

Luck didn't have much to do with his success, in my opinion. His commitment to learning and improving did.

But the plant shut down and he was out of a job. "I had to relocate myself and my family to a new city, but I did get another job within three months," he said. "And the pay actually was better. I know how lucky I am because most of my old buddies still are looking for work. And I'm continuing to take training courses in my new job."

GETTING READY TO LEARN

The plant manager is to be congratulated for his determination: When you hold a full-time job, have family responsibilities, and even want to have a few hours for fun and games, it's challenging also to attend classes and to study and prepare for them. Even if the courses you need and want are provided in-house by your employer on company time, and require no commuting on your part nor allocation of time that already is short, they still are work, and you have to be prepared for the slice of time they will take from your crowded day.

TAKING CHARGE OF YOUR EDUCATION

First figure out what you need and where and how to get it. Talk your plans over with your manager, friends, family, and career counselors. Include your projections in your one-year

You Can Do It

Whatever study you decide to undertake, you want to do the best in it you can, to always be prepared for classes, to participate in classroom discussion, and to get the best grade you can. Even if you managed to slide by in high school or college without doing much work, that no longer is an option. Continuing education is an important tool and you must keep it sharp. (I almost said give it your "awl.")

Don't keep your academic ambitions a secret. Make sure your bosses and colleagues know what you're doing. You won't be promoted simply because you have an additional credential, even if it's a doctorate. But you will be taken much more seriously as an important player at your work site. And that alone is worth the price of tuition.

plan and be realistic. (See Chapter 5.) You can't do everything at once. You don't want to set yourself up for failure. You might want to go slowly at first, taking only one course or seminar or workshop at a time. Remember, this is lifelong learning, and you will have a long life.

Visit the various educational institutions near your home. Find out what they can offer you. Talk to their career counselors and ask their help in scheduling your educational advancement. Don't make any quick decisions. Think everything over very carefully: You want to succeed in learning more. You don't want to find yourself exhausted, stressed out, and frustrated. You want to succeed—and you are the only one who can make sure that you will.

STARTING AT THE HIGH SCHOOL LEVEL

Many students are exploring career possibilities with their guidance counselors even before they are graduated from high school, some as early as sixth grade, and many wisely are opting for careers in technology and are making certain they take the courses they will need to qualify for a college major in their field of choice.

That's because it's almost impossible to do well unless you have that all-important high school diploma—something that even the most highly paid professional athletes know, with a

It's a fact of work life that you must have at least a high school diploma. It's the start of everything good!

handful of millionaire exceptions. For the rest of the world, though, a high school diploma is a must. Without it, you're not geared for success; you have little flexibility in what you can do and little chance of moving up the career ladder. And even if you are a Scout, if you don't complete high school you're not prepared.

A teacher who works with adult students in a computer and office-training program and who, in addition to teaching official skills, also helps her charges with their job searches and resumes, was concerned because they don't have a high school diploma—which most jobs available to them require. "They have plenty of experience but no education," she said. "What should I tell them to do?" Tell them to get that diploma. And if they want to move ahead in the field of computers, they will have to get more training and more degrees.

How to Get a High School Diploma

The good news in the world of education is that the high school graduate rate for U.S. students moved up slightly in 2000 to a record 86.5 percent, according to the U.S. Department of Education—an increase that reflects the fact that young Americans understand the importance of finishing at least 12 years of schooling. Though minority students' degree completion also increased, they lagged behind that of white students, something that is of great concern because of the increasingly diverse population that makes up of the nation's workforce. In tough times like these, young adults often bear the brunt of unemployment, according to research by economist Andrew Sum, director of Northeastern University's center for labor market studies. He has found that on average, during the months of September and October 2001—those fateful days—more than 555,000 fewer adults were employed. And to underscore the importance of a high school diploma, Sum also reports that "only 58 percent of young adults lacking a high school diploma or General Equivalency Diploma (GED) were employed."

The Department of Education's report also reflects the potency of having a GED because it includes GED holders in its research as high school graduates. A GED certificate is an extremely important certification—and an important tool—because being able to obtain one even after having dropped out of school gives workers without a K–12 diploma another chance to get one. And, according to the American Council on Education, more than 95 percent of U.S. employers consider GED graduates the same as traditional high school students when it comes to hiring, salary, and opportunities for advancement—in other words, everything that matters for a successful job hunt and career.

There are some 3,500 GED testing centers in 50 U.S. states, 9 U.S. territories and other areas, and 11 Canadian provinces. To find out how to qualify for a GED, ask about it at your local community college. Or contact the council's Center for Adult Learning at 202-939-9475. Web site address is www.acenet.edu/calec.

You Can Do It

When citing your credentials for a GED, don't forget to include your own personal achievements, such as speaking another language, volunteer work, and any projects you have worked on. They all can count.

EDUCATION BY DEGREES

"The economic recession, new or obsolete industries, and the quest to move up or just hang on to the career ladder have led more than 6 million adult students back to college this year," according to a report by Harper College, a community college in Palatine, Illinois. Bruce Bohrer, Harper's director of admission, emphasizes that "if you are thinking about making changes in your life and career . . . this is the place to come for help with answers to your questions." He expects a high turnout for the college's adult learning programs because of the events of September 11.

Lifelong learning is deeply rooted in community colleges throughout the United States, where adult development and growth are emphasized. And in addition to courses in your area of interest, the two-year associate degrees that these colleges offer often are what you need to qualify for a good job—and they also count toward the four-year baccalaureate degrees that open all doors.

In addition to associate degrees or certificates, other important areas of learning are vocational and trade schools, which provide a jump start for jobs for mechanics, hotel workers, automobile and air-conditioner repairers, travel agents, and aircraft technicians. (Warning: Check out these schools carefully with the Better Business Bureau and your state's attorney general before enrolling or paying tuition.)

Of course, a college degree is the number one credential for the best jobs. I for one thought that after the disasters of 9/11, potential college students would opt to stay close to home. I attended Temple University, just a bus and subway ride from my home in Philadelphia—and that was long before 2001. The truth is I couldn't afford to go to school away from home but there also was a certain security in commuting from my parents' house. Yet young people today are far more adventurous, and concern about being terrorist targets will not deter them from pursuing their education where they want to. "We're seeing applicants who are incredibly motivated, spirited self-starters, the type of kids for whom this kind of thing [the terrorist attacks] won't stop them,"

An undergraduate degree, whether one in business, science, or liberal arts, is the degree of choice for the best jobs with the brightest futures.

Jennifer G. Fondiller, dean of admissions at Barnard College in New York told *The New York Times*. If you don't have enough credits for a college degree or are thinking of working toward one, there's a possibility that over the years you've gained important knowledge and skills outside the classroom that you can get college credit for.

The College-Level Examination Program (CLEP) is a credit-by-examination program. Through it, according to Anne Messenger, who e-mailed me this information, 2,800 accredited colleges and universities award credit for satisfactory scores on CLEP examinations. For more information about CLEP, call 800-257-9558. E-mail address is clep@info.collegeboard.org.

ADVANCED DEGREES

An increasing number of professionals, such as social workers, librarians, business and financial professionals, accountants, human resource personnel, and even journalists, are finding they need a master's degree even to be considered for many jobs—and when it's not a requirement, it definitely is a

Most CEOs still believe if they want the most qualified people to run their companies, a job candidate with an MBA is the best bet.

door opener. And everyone knows the power of an MBA degree, in good times and in bad. Even though newly minted MBAs are not immune to a chaotic labor market, starting salaries remain high compared to those of other master's degree graduates—though perhaps not so astronomical today as they were in the 1990s. And opportunities, while reduced, are still plentiful.

MASTER'S AND DOCTORATE DEGREES

As much as I am a proponent of wall-to-wall education, in today's tough job market some problems concerning advanced degrees do arise that I want to warn you about. A former high school teacher with a master's degree in education wants to be a marketing assistant, but interviewers wonder why she isn't teaching when she has such an advanced degree. She wonders if she is too "overeducated" to get a job that doesn't require a master's degree. My advice to her is to leave off the master's degree in education from her resume but to bring it up as a badge of honor in the job interview. Specifically, I advise her to delineate all the ways her master's degree gives her added value as a marketing assistant, such as excellent communication skills, the ability to do extensive research, and firsthand knowledge of that all-important consumer market everyone wants to reach: teens.

I also give the same advice for those people fortunate enough to have doctorate degrees, a credential I highly endorse. If the job doesn't require one, don't mention it until the job interview. And then present it as an added advantage for both you and your employer. Though his doctorate has opened

Get all the education you can. Though there may be temporary setbacks, in the long run, it will pay off—and richly.

many doors for him and earned him a higher salary than colleagues without one, an electronic design engineer says when he applied for lesser jobs because of a slow economy the interview "came to a screeching halt" when the interviewer saw his advanced degree. "They assumed that when times get better, I'll be out the door," he told me. (What he does now is remove the Ph.D. from his resume and instead list his skills and achievements that apply to the job he wants, and he now is much more hopeful about getting one. Besides, he does have that mind-blowing education under his belt and no one can take it away from him.)

PROFESSIONAL ACCREDITATION, CERTIFICATION, AND LICENSING

More and more courses, workshops, seminars, and online learning are available for those who are serious about their career advancement and lifelong learning, such as those for Certified Professional Accountants, Board-Certified Physicians, Certified Work/Life Professionals, and Certified Auto Mechanics.

Every day, notices of new accreditations being offered by educational institutions and the professions themselves cross my desk. They expand the already myriad opportunities to enhance your skills. The Institute of Certified Travel Agents, for instance, offers professional certification. So does the Society for Human Resource Management. DePaul University now offers business organization and organizational development certificate programs. And many technical and vocational schools offer accreditation in information technology.

You Can Do It

Explore every avenue available to you that will prove a direct path to wherever you want to go in your career.

Many of these initiatives have been created specifically to help women and minorities who may not have been able to follow traditional paths in obtaining the credentials they need—a development that will benefit not only the continuing education student but the entire labor market in both quiet and turbulent times.

ONLINE INFORMATION

The means to find out what's available to you is right there at your fingertips: your personal computer. Use it. "I want to take a particular course that has nothing to do with my present job but interests me greatly and might possibly facilitate a career change," an executive assistant told me. "I need to know a lot more before I do anything, but I can't ask any questions at work because they would know I'm planning to do something different and possibly leave my present job. I can't afford to lose my job. What can I do?"

What she can do is turn to the Internet to find answers to her questions. Frances E. Roehm, a librarian at the Skokie, Illinois, Public Library and Webmaster of www.chicagojobs.org, is the personification of the description of a librarian as the "original search engine."

GETTING STARTED

I asked Roehm, an online whiz, to search the Internet for some helpful sources for adult lifelong learning. Here's what she recommends:

> **Back to College Resources for Re-entry Students.** For re-entry students. Access at: www.back2college.com.

> **FirstGov for Workers.** Connects American workers and their families to government services and information, including training, certificate programs, community colleges, and four-year colleges and universities. Access at: www.workers.gov.

Send Your Child to College. The Internet guide for parents. Access at: www.guideforparents.com.

Think College. Learn for a lifetime! Includes information for returning students, from GED on up. Access at: www.ed.gov/thinkcollege.

Certification and Professional Development

America's CareerInfoNet. Click on Licensed Occupations to find licensing requirements by state, occupation, or agency. Access at: www.acinet.org/acinet/lois_start.htm.

Directories of Accreditation Associations. Access at: www.chea.org/directories.

Kaplan Inc. Links to professional development and test preparatory materials for some professions, among them insurance and real estate. Access at: www.kaplan.com.

The Riley Guide. Certification and licensing information. Access at: www.rileyguide.com/certif.html.

Directories of Colleges and Universities

American Association of Community Colleges. Access at: www.aacc.nche.edu.

Peterson's. Guide to secondary education and adult distance learning. Access at: www.petersons.com.

U.S. News Education. Information about colleges and universities. Access at: www.usnews.com/usnews/edu/eduhome.htm.

Online Courses

Degree.net. Features material related to distance education and nontraditional degrees. Access at: www.degree.net.

Peterson's. Click on distance learning programs for courses by content or institutional name. Access at: www.petersons.com.

You Can Do It

Continuing and continuous education will help you achieve the lifestyle you want. (Make sure that the courses you sign up for, especially online, are accredited.) Lifelong learning is one of the factors involved in the highly desired goal of balancing your professional and personal lives. In Chapter 7, I'll show you how it's possible to achieve that balance—even when jobs are scarce.

SmartPlanet. More than 600 information technology online courses. Access at: www.zdnet.com/smartplanet.

The World Lecture Hall. Has more than 100 categories of educational material. Access at: www.vcu.edu/mdcweb/english.

Nondegree Programs

Element K. Online professional training. Access at: www.elementk.com.

Massachusetts Institute of Technology Open-CourseWare. MIT offers undergraduate and graduate course material free. Access at: http://web.mit.edu/ocw/

OnlineLearning.net. This Sylvan Learning company offers some certificate programs through partnerships with UCLA and the University of San Diego. Access at: www.onlinelearning.net.

Specific Fields

Association of Social Work Boards. Access at: www.aswb.org.

Human Resource Certification Institute. Access at: www.hrci.org.

State Child Care Regulatory Offices. Access at: www.nccic.org/dirs/regoffic.html.

For other professional associations offering certification, accreditation, or advanced seminars, librarian Roehm recommends going to the library and using the *Encyclopedia of Associations* (Gale Group). Another good source is the search engine Google. Access at: www.google.com.

chapter 7

HAVING A JOB AND A LIFE, TOO

I t's understandable in today's uncertain labor market for you to settle for less pay and responsibility and even to take a so-called "lesser" job. In fact, these could be very smart moves to make, especially if you get hungry three times a day. (See Chapter 3.) But the one area I strongly urge you to be steadfast about—short of being demanding or confrontational—is when it comes to meeting your own personal requirements of quality of life.

Making sure you have personal satisfaction—even if it's time off to run a marathon or play tennis or golf—is too important to your well-being and happiness for you to forgo it. Even though I don't advise trying to drive too hard a bargain when it comes to salary negotiations and definitely want to discourage you here and now from complaining too vigorously about small raises, salary freezes, or shortage of office supplies, I emphatically urge you to negotiate with as much confidence as you can muster, considering what's at stake, for the working arrangements that make you happy and are as stress-free as possible.

> ## *You Can Do It*
>
> What I'm talking about is a life after 5 P.M. and even before then. And weekends, too. These are chaotic times, as I've frequently pointed out, and in order to get through them—and they will pass—you need a balanced life, one with flexibility, one with time to spend with family and friends, to fulfill your responsibilities outside work, and to nourish your hopes and dreams of what you will do when you live in a peaceful world.

NEW ATTITUDES OF EMPLOYEES

The events of September 11 and a declining economy have changed how employees think and feel. They're looking for greater meaning in their lives and that will now include greater flexibility in their schedules, which might entail working from home or having more personal days, more vacation days, and overall more time off to spend with family and friends.

Every day, Americans are reevaluating their lives after the shock of the terrorist attacks that permanently affected all of

> ## *You Can Do It*
>
> If you want your life to be less restrictive because of work demands, you have to do what it takes to get what you want. And that could include switching your job to one where the hours give you the freedom to be able to perform well professionally and also to have time for yourself and your personal needs and responsibilities. Or to a company that is known to deliver on its promise of being both employee and family friendly. It's up to you. And it's called self-determination.

us—and additional time with our families and friends is high on the list of millions of employees, especially the ones, like me, who only wanted to run home and hug and kiss their kids on September 11. To many of us, in the wake of such world-shattering events, it seems ridiculous to have to work 12-hour days and work on weekends when we realize we have only limited hours to live our lives—and even that, of course, no longer is a given.

EMPLOYERS' CONCERNS

Though most business, government, and nonprofit organizations are focusing on how to save money (too often, I believe, the easy answer is to lay off employees) they also are concerned about how to retain their best workers, who often make up a skeleton staff of workers after massive downsizings. And one of the answers is to offer work/life benefits. A survey of 481 benefits and compensation staff by MetLife shows that 58 percent of employers see programs that help workers achieve balance as one of their most important strategies when it comes to retention (recruitment no longer being the major problem it was before September 11).

Despite operating in a less secure world, employers still are conducting employee surveys to find out what employees

You Can Do It

Uncertain times make everyone more introspective, more focused on the things that really matter. And the one value most Americans are talking about today is quality time for themselves and their families. Just because you have a job doesn't mean you have to become a workaholic—or to remain being one if that's been your pattern—to keep your job even when employment opportunities no longer are plentiful.

want and need and to ascertain not only their work values but also their personal values. And what do employees want? Time to do their jobs well and time for themselves.

HOW WORK/LIFE BALANCE WAS BORN

The idea that you can have a job, advance your career, and still handle your family responsibilities is a direct result of the influx of women in the paid labor market, which began in the 1970s. Men long had the advantage of having a spouse at home full-time to take care of all household and family responsibilities, but the huge number of women working full-time and part-time turned that around. The women's movement that swept the country focused on issues such as child care, flexible hours, and sharing of family responsibilities in the home.

Since women are such needed and valuable workers—despite the lack of their presence among top executive officers and as company directors, which we know as the glass ceiling—employers responded, albeit slowly, to feminist pressure with supportive programs that helped women stay in the labor market without sacrificing their children's needs.

At the same time, men, also sensitized to the fact that children need fathers, too, began to ask for flexible hours, time off to attend parent-teacher meetings, to be Soccer Dads while their wives were Soccer Moms, to enjoy their children's childhood, and to relax a bit themselves. In this way, work/life balance has become a way of life for women and men alike, even though women still are the majority of users of company-sponsored work/life benefits.

Other groups are tuned in to the promise of a balanced life: A majority of undergraduates name it as their top career goal; single people say they have a right to it, too; Generation Y, the 29 million Americans born from 1981 and on, are extremely vocal about making the demands of their work lives fit the demands of their personal lives, and deserve our admiration for sticking to their standards of what makes life worth living.

Executives, too, whose spouses now also work full-time,

You Can Do It

Both women and men have the right to be able to be there when their families need them and the right to have enough leisure time to enjoy life. A balanced life is a firewall against stress, which impairs employees both at work and in their personal lives. Dissatisfaction on the job and unhappiness outside the office are intimately entwined.

also want a life. A study by Lewis PR shows that 82 percent of marketing directors "struggle to get the balance right between their professional and private lives." And you know that when executives start talking about balance, they'll soon implement it for themselves and everyone else—and the most successful work/life programs come with the endorsement and implementation from the top down.

DOING SOMETHING ABOUT IT

"Doing your homework," one of my favorite bits of advice, also encompasses learning all you can about work/life benefits. Find out everything your company offers by checking your

You Can Do It

You have to be proactive about obtaining the work/life benefits you want to make your life a full and happy one. As in many other things in today's job market—in fact, in today's world—it's all up to you. And the way to make it happen is first to know what you legitimately can ask for and then to have a strategy to achieve your goals.

employee handbook, talking to your manager, and asking your human resources department. Check out at your local library or on the Internet the many lists of companies that really care about their employees; see what they have, what fits your needs, and whether any of their programs could be introduced at your company. (And whether they have any job openings!) Ask your colleagues what they need and want to make their lives whole. Talk to your manager about your needs. Compile your own I-Must-Have list.

YOUR MENU OF PROTECTIVE LAWS AND WORK ARRANGEMENTS

Happily, there are a variety of opportunities and options to bring some balance into your life without losing your job.

Family and Medical Leave Act

This is perhaps the most important employment legislation passed in recent years. In 1993, FMLA was signed into law. It mandates entitlement of 12 weeks of unpaid leave each year for employees—and that means both women and men who work for organizations with 50 or more workers.

The key words here are "unpaid," which employee advocates are trying to change to "paid," and "50 or more workers," which avid supporters of work/life balance are trying to change to "15 or more." To qualify, you must have worked for your employer for at least 1,250 hours for one year preceding the leave.

It guarantees that you will have a job when you return from caring for your newborn, adopted child, or sick family member or from your own health problem that prevented you from working. It also continues your health and other benefits during your leave and protects your seniority, all of which really makes the difference between simply being able to not show up for work when you cannot and being able to maintain your financial security and job status.

Plan for your leave as far ahead of time as you can. Offer a plan for how your work can be done and who can do it (coworkers or hiring of temporary workers since your leave is unpaid and not costing the company anything). Give the date you want to leave, if possible. Government research shows that the percentage of women working during pregnancy before their first birth increased to 67 percent in the early 1990s from 44 percent in the early 1960s, according to the U.S. Bureau of the Census. Today, working as long as you can before giving birth is on the rise because doing so means the new mother has more time under FMLA to spend at home. If your leave is not sudden, as is usually the case with pregnancies, make sure your exit date is okay with your manager. Also list the date you plan to return. Be sure to find out in advance if you have to use up all your vacation time and other days due before FMLA kicks in. Above all, remember you have a legal right to this leave.

Part-Time Work

Reducing your workweek to less than a full-time job has long been a viable solution for people who do not want to work full-time or cannot find a full-time job. In today's economy, part-time work is plentiful (while full-time jobs are not), because these jobs usually do not provide health insurance or other benefits. Still, part-time work, including working for a temporary agency, is an important option for those who want to continue earning some income, to keep their experience up-to-date, to be on the "inside" of a company—and to have time for their other interests and responsibilities.

If you're currently working full-time and want to reduce your hours to part-time, devise a plan of how this can be done and how the work can still be accomlished before you approach your manager about the possible switch. Make sure you have a track record of excellent performance before making your request.

Flexible Hours

So many people have told me that either scaling back their work hours or devising a flexible work schedule is the best thing that ever happened to them. Where is it written that everyone must work from 9 A.M. to 5 P.M. every day? Certainly not on the expressway! I've never really understood why managers depend so much on "face time" and feel secure only when employees are directly under their thumbs. Being able to see the employee all day long doesn't mean the work is getting done. And handling a full workload with flexibility, being able to work the hours and times that also allow you to meet your personal needs, has been proven to increase employee productivity.

Flexible scheduling is another result of the influx of women into the labor market and their need for customized scheduling in full-time jobs. Today, most companies accept this as another viable way to work, provided the work gets done. Flexible hours, which have been slowly evolving, can mean working 10 hours a day four days a week (compressed time).

It can mean coming in a little later so you can get the kids off to school and leaving a little earlier to be there when they get home—but forgoing lunch hours and/or coming in weekends to complete assignments.

It can mean job sharing, in which two people do one job and share pay, benefits, and responsibilities. The typical arrangement is that each person works two days with one day overlapping. Many employers tell me when they allow employees to job share, they often find they have two full-time employees 24 hours every day, instead of just one for eight hours, because the job shares are so responsible.

Some people, such as accountants and lawyers, make arrangements to work seasonally, when demand for their services is highest or special projects need to be done. Seasonal work means earning less money on a year-round basis, although some studies show salaries for the weeks worked are surprisingly good. But seasonal work allows you to stay on a career track with hours that are self-determined. Most workers do not start out with flexible hours; most have to prove themselves on the job. It usually takes one year, though you can ask for the arrangement you want when hired and show that the work will get done without hands-on management.

Being able to get flextime means earning your manager's

support. It seems to be easier for women to get flexible sched-uling than for men; working fathers usually are only grudg-ingly given permission to vary their work hours. But clearly, flexible hours are not only a women's issue. Men need them, too. If possible, ask to try your proposed schedule on a trial ba-sis for three months. That gives both you and your manager time to work out the glitches and to ascertain whether both of you want to continue with it.

Devising the schedule of the hours you want to work, keeping in touch with your colleagues and managers, and planning what you will do each day should be your responsi-bility, subject to the manager's approval: If the flex schedule doesn't serve enough of your needs, it's not worth doing. And ask for a review of your arrangement every six months.

In my opinion, flexible hours are the greatest hope for workers to have a life. In fact, there is a consulting and staffing firm, Flexible Resources, Inc., based in Cos Cob, Connecticut, that specializes in—and makes a living from—placing women and men in nontraditional work arrangements, most of them full-time jobs. When someone makes money from employers willing to pay them to find employees for them who work in jobs with flexible schedules, you know there's a future in this way of scheduling work!

Telecommuting: Moving Work to the Workers

Working from home is not only prevalent, it's a fact of life in today's workplace—or, actually, outside of it. And it's made possible by the new technology that adds to the advantage of having a telephone to communicate with clients, colleagues, and managers the extra abilities engendered by fax machines, computers, cell phones, beepers, laptops, e-mail, Internet ac-cess, duplicating machines, and scanners.

Technology professionals were among the first to say to heck with commuting and to question the purpose of spend-ing long hours getting to and from work when their jobs could be done so easily on computers at home. According to *Recruiting Trends* newsletter, "A whopping 96 percent of 1,953 techies surveyed indicate they want to work from home at least a few hours every week, and 39 percent say they'd take a pay cut to be able to telecommute." Now, of course, millions of U.S. workers see the advantages of telecommuting: Virtual offices and virtual teams have been on the increase since the terrorist attacks of September 11 because more workers feel safer working at home than working in highly visible offices and, as ever, also want more time to bask in the comfort of their families.

To the telecommuter, working from home even only part of the week means saving time getting dressed up and commuting, and saving the expense of both. The stereotypical picture of a telecommuter sounds lovely to me: Working in your jammies and bathrobe and even wearing comfortable bunny slippers. It also can mean being able to get your kids off to school, greet them when they come home, work in various medical and school appointments, shop when the supermarket isn't crowded—and still get your work done. That's the ideal, of course, although it still is a very demanding schedule to have. And it's important to keep in mind that telecommuting does have its problems.

Many telecommuters tell me they don't advance as rapidly in their careers as their full-time, face-time colleagues. Others report family members don't believe they're really working and feel free to interrupt them whenever they want to, despite having dedicated offices and phone lines. Another major problem is the fact that managers often are skeptical of how much work telecommuters actually do. And the most exasperating problem, I'm told, is that the unspoken expectation is that if you are able to get permission, you lucky you, to work from home, you're on call to your bosses and clients 24 hours a day. Many telecommuters tell me it is very hard to limit themselves to only an eight-hour day when the work always is there—and so are they.

To make telecommuting work for you, make sure you're in good standing with your manager before requesting it. Discuss in advance how you will do the work at home. Ask for the company to install and pay for all needed equipment, including fax paper and other supplies (your company can write it off). Arrange to come into the office at least once a

You Can Do It

Having control over your hours is only one-half of having a life. The other half is doing a good job.

week and for all important meetings. Stress your eagerness to be available through frequent e-mail messages to the office and conference calls.

If you want to succeed as a remote worker, be familiar with your company's guidelines on the subject—or help write them! You should not have to pay a penalty for not always being visible, so set up weekly or monthly discussions (these can be virtual, too) with your manager for evaluations and reevaluations. Remember, you're the one who wanted this arrangement, so make sure it works. In order to be successful, be sure you fully understand that your work from home is serious work and deserves your full professional attention.

BENEFITS YOU WANT TO ENJOY

In addition to helpful work arrangements, there are many benefits companies offer to help you get through the day with a peace of mind that allows you to focus on the job you are doing.

Child Care

This benefit, which employers can implement, includes (1) onsite child care, a very costly program even though employees pay to use it, but one that pays off richly for parents and children; (2) paid or partially paid child care at an outside facility that the company might have a vested interest in; and (3) child care referral services that help workers find quality, low-cost, and convenient child care.

Some forward-looking companies also reach out to care-givers in the community and help them to become licensed child care providers. Many have summer programs for children of employees and offer child care options when the children are sick or there are school vacation days. And dependent care spending accounts, a federal tax program, are an option easily provided by employers for workers with young children.

Elder Care

Baby boomers and even their children's generation, Genera-tion Xers, have elderly parents who need care. On-site elder care, help with paying for elder care at an outside facility, and elder care referral services are extremely helpful—and well used by employees. Workers in the sandwich generation—caught between children who need day care and elderly parents who need elder care—find that the responsibilities are completely different ones, with elder care, they report, being far more de-manding and stressful because it usually is so unpredictable.

Sabbaticals

College and university professors, particularly those with tenure, have long enjoyed this perk. Recently, private organi-zations and businesses also have been offering it to employ-ees. It most often is offered to employees who have been with the company five years and also usually is a paid leave of from three months to one year. It's a time of renewal and even recovery for many exhausted workers, who typically re-turn to work after the long absence with renewed vigor and commitment.

Wellness Programs and Fitness Centers

On-site facilities or paid or partially paid memberships in out-side facilities are a very popular benefit savvy companies are offering to relieve stress and to keep workers fit. Executives, particularly top ones, are enthusiastic about having a place to work out, play basketball, or swim because that's what they themselves like to do.

Being able to do your job and at the same time feel fulfilled as a human being with a personal life is possible if employers are sincere in helping to make it happen.

Volunteering

One of the most satisfying benefits a company can provide is to allow employees time off to volunteer and to arrange their participation in company-sponsored volunteer efforts. Many employers know that one of the barriers to employees participating in volunteer activities is that they simply don't have time, despite the new emphasis on giving back and helping others that was precipitated by the terrorist attacks. And that's why employer-approved and sponsored volunteering now has a new aspect: family volunteering. Many of the programs now involve not only workers but also their families and friends and allow them to spend valuable time together doing something for someone else.

Volunteering can also be beneficial to job seekers. As a volunteer, you meet people you can network with—and you might meet your future employer or a source that leads you to your future employer!

AND NOW FOR THE EXTRAS

Since 1998 I've been writing the "WorkLife" column for *The Chicago Tribune*, the only weekly nationally syndicated column on work/life issues (my two other weekly columns are about jobs). While covering my beat for "WorkLife," I've accumulated a list of some of the most wonderful employee benefits I've ever heard of. I'd love to have all of them for myself, even the ones involving employees' automobiles, even though I don't have a car!

Today's employers are open to creative solutions that help employees successfully juggle all the elements of their lives. Come up with a few ideas of your own, research them, and present them!

Some of the winners include dry-cleaning services, auto tune-ups and washing at reduced rates, tickets for theater and sporting events, discounted travel arrangements, transportation and commuting discounts, catalog purchases at lower rates, massages in your office at your desk, catering services with meals to bring home, permission to bring pets to the office, financial and retirement planning, organized sports activities, pinball machines, rooms to relax in at work (not the washroom), and necessities such as lactation rooms, lactation consultants, and well baby clinics.

Two programs I've run across are especially creative. One allows employees to "buy" or "sell" up to four vacation days a year, a benefit that unfortunately is offered by only a handful of employers. Here's how it works: At firms where all paid time off is put into a pool, employees can "buy" additional time off without pay. And when they "sell," they get actual cash to use as they wish. Both options must have management approval.

Another type of activity that makes sense because of its positive impact on morale and on retention is that of providing employees fun things to do at no cost to the employee—and doing them as a group. One telecommunications company involved in this offers cooking lessons with a certified chef, bowling, playing arcade games together, and even marching in parades. Everyone, even the top executives, join in.

THE FUTURE OF WORK/LIFE BENEFITS

In slow economic times, employers focus more intently than ever on the bottom line and try to cut expenses wherever

A soft economy doesn't mean that all work/life benefits are in jeopardy. It does mean that employers very carefully are scrutinizing the programs they offered when times were very good and are trying to analyze their worth.

they can. First to go are employees in massive downsizings that continue on and on. Next, salaries are frozen or reduced. And soon after that benefits and other so-called "perks" that are considered "luxuries" by some employers are deep-sixed. Yet, I have observed that very few companies are pulling the plug on work/life benefits and flexible hours. Those that have done this got immediate and loud howls of complaint from workers and now understand the programs that make it possible for employees to get their jobs done and to have a life, too, are part of the fabric of the American workplace—and can't be cut just like that, without preparation, explanations, and even apologies. Even in tough economic times, the Boss cannot giveth in this area and then so easily taketh away.

THE CONTINUING NEED FOR WORK/LIFE BENEFITS

Work/life benefits, I believe, are here to stay. One example of their stability is the profession of work/life consultants and practitioners. This relatively new career field definitely is on the rise, as shown through the establishment of The Alliance of Work/Life Professionals. Founded in 1996, it offers certificate courses to members through classes offered by Boston College, and the Alliance plans soon to certify its members. All these developments are indications that the work these professionals do is important—and in demand.

Despite the increase in unemployment, employers still are

There's no reason to be chained to your desk all day at the office or plant when there are so many work/life balance options that can help you enrich your life.

slow to cut back on flexibility, because it doesn't cost them anything. What may be taking a hit, however, are benefits that the company pays for in full or in part. Many of these benefits are the things the wife used to do when the husband was the sole support of the family. They include child care, laundry and cleaning, taking kids to and from school, elder care, referral services, and more. But now most adult women are in paid employment.

Although some benefits consulting firms such as Winning Workplaces, a nonprofit organization, are showing employers how to offer these programs at no cost or very low cost (a dry cleaning service, for instance, might not charge anything or might even pay the company for the opportunity to do business on-site), the employers' help with replacing so-called "women's work" is not expected to expand in a slow economy. But flexible scheduling, which is viewed as directly contributing to the bottom line, isn't expected to suffer as much. Instead, flexible hours and self-scheduling might even be expanded to relieve stress felt by the remaining and overworked staff at downsized companies nationwide.

So don't hesitate to request a reduced workweek and to negotiate the hours. Today, with a little bit of luck and perseverance, you'll get what you want!

TAKING CHARGE

Just as it's up to you to be proactive about finding a new job or climbing up the career ladder, you must also take respon-

You Can Do It

You deserve to have a wonderful job, a fulfilling life, and some inner peace despite world turmoil. It's up to you. I know you can do it, and in Chapter 8 I'll summarize what's necessary for you to do to be there and do that.

sibility for having a satisfying life. Very few employers will come to you and say, "What a nice person you are. We want you to work for us forever. Just tell us what will make you happy and we will give it you." It simply doesn't work that way. And that's why so many employees are taking time to analyze what it is they need and what they can do about getting it. It's a sure way of having a satisfying life and of reducing stress.

chapter **8**

YOU CAN DO IT

Now is the time to talk about success. Yours. The word "success" has several different definitions, according to *Webster's New World Dictionary*:

- The first is "a favorable result."

- The second, "the gaining of wealth and fame."

- The third is "a successful person or thing."

- And I would add a fourth: "an achievement that is not necessarily elusive, even in chaotic times."

Your success—gaining "a favorable result"—in looking for a job or keeping and advancing in the one you now have is at your fingertips.

In the previous chapters of this book, you've been thoroughly schooled in the information you need about where the jobs actually are and how to get the one you want. And you've also been informed about how to be outstanding in your present position in order to keep your job and then to take the next step up in your career.

You now also have a handle on "the gaining of wealth,"

152

though not necessarily "fame." In this book, I've shown you how to negotiate a salary. And the vital information about what the top jobs actually pay can be found in Chapters 9 and 10. The third definition, being "a successful person," is something everyone in the labor market (which includes those who are employed and also those who are looking for jobs) aspires to. In previous chapters, I've given you inside tips on how to gauge what you want to do and how to evaluate what you're doing. And, of course, my own personal definition of success also includes having time for myself (for tennis, especially) and my family (for my three children and four grandchildren). In that, I'm no different from anyone else.

I am someone who believes you deserve a boss who understands that at any given moment you may want to go kayaking in Kauai—and you deserve the time off. And to elaborate on my own definition of success as something that can be achieved even in a slow labor market, I urge you to go for the gold and not let economic conditions temper your dreams. In other words, no matter what's happening in the world, especially matters not under your control, hang in there.

Go for it. Taking the measure of success is an individual process; there is no standard rule for everyone. But right now the one item that should be on your agenda, the one thing that should be of major concern to you, is the state of your career. And well it should be. That's why I want to emphasize some of the critical points in gaining that success, whatever your definition of it, for yourself—which might result not only in fortune but perhaps even in fame!

You Can Do It

Your career can take you for the ride of your life, the one you've always wanted to take, despite twists and turns and detours—but only if you are the one in charge of steering it.

YOUR OWN PERSONAL MEASURE OF SUCCESS

The possibilities of making it to the top are many. And when I talk about the "top," I don't mean only the very top, the hallowed ranks of CEOs and other major movers and shakers. That's because success is there to be achieved at every level of your career ladder, and the rung you pick as your goal is your own personal measure of success. I agree with Bruce Tulgan and Carolyn Martin, coauthors of *Managing Generation Y*, that the "voices of these young entrants [born in the late 1970s and early 1980s] to the labor market 'ring out loud and true.' " And one of the messages that resonate is that they are not afraid to claim success for themselves measured by their own definitions of it.

"Gen Yers are not only outside-the-box thinkers; they are innovative over-the-wall doers who won't settle for one-size-fits-all solutions," Tulgan and Martin write. And that is why, they conclude, "Gen Yers unrelentingly ask you, 'Why'?" The big Why of success means never having to say you're sorry, but you do have to keep questioning yourself and respected—and friendly—managers, colleagues, and even clients about how your efforts are going, in their eyes, to get your career on that fast track, in order to understand the challenges and the possibilities of what you want to do and make the right moves in the way to a satisfying career.

Taking the pulse of your progress toward success is an important part of the process of achieving it. I suggested earlier, in Chapter 3, in reference to the conclusion of your job interview, that it's okay to ask the potential employer, "How did I do?" Now I suggest you ask, "How am I doing?" in reference to your efforts to make your career a success. You'll learn a lot from the answers.

A DIFFICULT LESSON

You also have to learn a lesson that often is difficult to comprehend: You must recognize that when roadblocks arise that you simply can't do anything about you will have to take a de-

You Can Do It

The reality of getting and keeping a job, no matter what is happening in the economy or the labor market, means that you probably won't succeed in absolutely everything you want to do or excel in every one of your career endeavors—although I hope you do. But just to be on the safe side I want to suggest that the wisest way to approach your successful career is in the manner of the proverbial American porcupine, also known as a hedgehog, when it is making love: very carefully. That also means: Don't make quick decisions. Don't rush to judgment. Don't lose your head when faced with nitty-gritty career situations. Don't despair. Instead, face what I know will be your successful professional life with enthusiasm—and a sense of humor.

tour—but you will not have to retrace all your steps and start all over again. That's because knowledge is power, and with all you've learned about the ins and outs of the job market, the importance of continuing education, the necessity to network, and your own confidence to have both a life and job, your feet are firmly planted on the ladder of success, with only the sky as your limit.

MANAGING YOUR SUCCESS

The American Management Association (AMA), based in New York, is a nonprofit organization I have long respected because it has a record of being on the cutting edge of change. An unapologetic enthusiast for lifelong learning, the AMA holds training seminars that are always profitable for the managers who take them. But you don't have to be a manager to benefit from the association's unerring approach to success. In a recent list of 150 seminars provided through its Learning for Life program (for more information see www.amanet.org/7K5), the AMA's emphasis is on "the skills you need in business today."

And I, for one, think these skills apply to everyone who wants to have a successful career. The workshops and training sessions include these 13 basics for success: communication skills, finance, human resource training, information technology, interpersonal skills, leadership, management, marketing, process management, project management, purchasing management, sales/customer service, and strategic management. If you're a manager, you will immediately see the importance of each of these educational programs in supervising a staff and increasing productivity. If you don't manage people, you will immediately see that you can apply each of these subjects to the management of the most important employee you know: yourself.

Here's how I have connected the 13 AMA training topics to the skills necessary for your personal success:

1. How well you communicate determines how quickly you will move ahead.

2. Being able to handle your own financial matters, including your individual negotiations for salary and benefits, is essential to advancing your career.

3. You will be judged by your familiarity with your company's human resource policies and your ability to meet its expectations of you as an employee.

4. Your knowledge of information technology, continually updated, is a basic tool for your personal and professional requirements for success in today's technological society.

5. Having finely honed interpersonal skills means you can get along well with both management, staff, and particularly your team members.

6. Leadership skills on a personal level mean stepping in when necessary and offering suggestions or even taking

charge unofficially—until the day when you actually do take charge.

7. Management means taking charge of your career in a proactive and well-informed way.

8. Marketing means aggressively (but not too aggressively) promoting and selling yourself to the company and your colleagues to show you're a serious player with serious ambition.

9. Getting your arms around process management means you understand firsthand what is involved in getting your next promotion or your next choice assignment— and working to make sure you're considered for both.

10. Project management means creating for yourself and working by yourself on projects that, when completed, will enhance your value to the company. An example: taking responsibility for supplying information, with your manager's approval, to your company's web site about your department's achievements.

11. Purchasing management, as it relates to your career, is knowing and making sure you have the tools you need to be successful in your present job, including electronic equipment, support staff, training, and continuing education.

12. Sales/customer service means being knowledgeable about the market you are serving and understanding the needs of the consumers you are trying to sell to. In addition, on a personal level, it means being aware of the needs of

You Can Do It

In this post–September 11 world of work, you, like many others, may realize your career priorities have shifted. Be in touch with what matters to you.

your supervisors and doing whatever you can to meet those needs.

13. Strategic management is exactly that: Develop a strategy to manage your career—and follow it. Strategically.

SHIFTING PRIORITIES

Success at work isn't enough for a well-rounded life or to reach the nirvana of life: happiness. Your personal time and your personal life also matter, even in recessionary times. "When it comes to family matters, job seekers and workers are shifting priorities," says Carlo Martellotti, regional vice president of Drake Beam Morin's Midwest area. DBM is a global human resource consulting firm based in New York. "[They are] placing higher value on working less and spending more time with family and friends, making life choices over career choices." And Martellotti adds: "Life clearly is different for everyone than it was [before September 11]. We're pleased to see a growing optimism that the worst is over and it's time to start anew. Job seekers as well as employers have learned some hard yet valuable lessons."

A FINAL WORD ABOUT SUCCESS

Your aim is to get and keep a job you really want. Hopefully, I've given you some insights into what it takes to be successful in that endeavor. Once again, I want to emphasize the basics of

You Can Do It

Events beyond our control changed the world we live in. Our ability to adapt and to be flexible will determine how successful we are as citizens of the twenty-first century.

You Can Do It

Now is the time to realize that the future isn't a hazy moment several years down the road. It's here now. Make it work for you.

career survival in uncertain economic times. Here's what you want to be sure you have:

- An updated resume.
- Strong networking contacts.
- A mentor.
- Transferable skills.
- Continuing education.
- Open communication with managers and colleagues.
- A life.

ADDED VALUE INFORMATION

See Chapter 9 for a listing of the best technical jobs with salaries and skill requirements.

See Chapter 10 for a listing of the best professional jobs and more—also with salaries and skill requirements.

You can do it!

The Cutting Edge: The Best Computer Technology and Engineering Jobs

Computer and Information Systems Managers
Computer, Automated Teller, and Office Machine Repairers
Computer Engineers
Computer Programmers
Computer Support Specialists and Systems Administrators
Data Entry and Information Processing Workers
Desktop Publishers
Drafters
Engineers
Semiconductor Processors
Systems Analysts, Computer Scientists, and
    Database Administrators

The material in this chapter comes from the Bureau of Labor Statistics (U.S. Department of Labor's *Occupational Outlook Handbook* and America's CareerInfoNet).

COMPUTER AND INFORMATION SYSTEMS MANAGERS

Job Skills and Requirements: Computer and information systems managers, including chief technology officers and management of information systems (MIS) directors, plan, coordinate, direct, research, design, and evaluate firms' computer-related activities. Bachelor's degree typically is required, but employers often prefer master's degree in business administration with heavy emphasis on information technology. Strong technical and business skills are required, with experience in software and business management or consulting. Strong interpersonal, communication, and leadership skills are important to interact with employees, top management, and customers. A keen understanding of people, processes, and customers' needs is required.

Salary Range: $78,830 to $81,983.

☞ *Inside Track:* Strong job opportunities stem from technical advancements and rapid growth among computer-related occupations. More job openings will result from the need to replace managers who retire or move into other occupations. The exploding growth of the Internet and e-commerce will make computer and information systems managers more vital to companies to stay competitive. Management position is best obtained by workers who possess an MBA and have advanced technical knowledge, business expertise, and strong communication and administrative skills. There will be a high demand for managers proficient in computer security issues, as organizations focus importance on protecting their systems from hackers, viruses, and other acts of cyberterrorism. Managers often receive more benefits than nonmanagerial workers, including expense accounts, bonuses, and stock option plans.

COMPUTER, AUTOMATED TELLER, AND OFFICE MACHINE REPAIRERS

Job Skills and Requirements: Computer, automated teller machine (ATM), and office machine repairers perform hands-on repair, maintenance, and installation of computers and related equipment. Employers prefer workers certified as repairers or who have training in electronics from associate degree programs, the military, vocational schools, or equipment manufacturers. Electronics knowledge is necessary, and strong diagnostic, problem-solving, and technical skills are required. Good communications skills are important for repairers who interact with clients or work in a shop.

Salary Range: $31,366 to $32,614.

☞ *Inside Track:* As businesses increasingly depend on computers and other sophisticated machines, the need to maintain this equipment will create new jobs for repairers, with computer repair as one of the fastest growing jobs. Prospects are best for applicants with repair experience and knowledge in electronics and mechanical equipment. Employers generally provide new repairers some training on specific equipment, but workers are expected to arrive on the job with a basic understanding of repair. The job involves some physical activity as repairers may be lifting equipment and working in a variety of postures. Because computers, ATMs, and office machines are critical for businesses to function efficiently, repairers often work around the clock, including weekends and holidays.

COMPUTER ENGINEERS

Job Skills and Requirements: Computer engineers research, design, develop, test, and evaluate the hardware or software of computer systems. Most employers prefer to hire people who have at least a bachelor's degree and computer knowledge and experience. Degree concentrations typically are computer science, information systems or software, or electronics engineering. For jobs that don't require computer-related degrees, training programs are offered by systems software vendors, including Microsoft, Novell, and Oracle, and professional certification is offered by several organizations, including the Institute for Certification of Computing Professionals. Computer engineers need strong programming, problem-solving, and analytical skills and must be detail-oriented, with good interpersonal skills to communicate with coworkers and customers. As technology rapidly evolves, acquiring new skills through continuing education and professional development is critical.

Salary Ranges: Computer software engineers $67,670 to $70,377. Computer hardware engineers $67,300 to $69,992.

☞ *Inside Track:* Computer engineer is one of the highest-paying and fastest-growing jobs, with the most openings projected through 2008. Spurring growth are the Internet, e-mail, and e-commerce, which require computer engineering skills to build and manage Web content and infrastructures, as well as companies' need to create and maintain complex technology-based systems to stay competitive. Employers range from start-ups and nonprofits to corporations and governments. Students seeking computer engineering jobs increase employment opportunities by participating in internships and co-op programs offered through schools. Inexperienced college graduates gain advantage through training and certification programs, including those offered by employers. Computer engineers may have to work long hours, as well as evenings and weekends, to meet project deadlines or handle unexpected technical problems.

COMPUTER PROGRAMMERS

Job Skills and Requirements: Computer programmers write, test, and maintain in a logical manner the detailed instructions, or software programs, that tell the computer what to do. Bachelor's degree in computer science, mathematics, or information systems typically is required, although programmers may qualify for certain jobs with two-year degrees, training programs, or certificates. Graduate degree is needed for advanced applications. Business skills and experience are helpful. Employers typically seek computer programming knowledge or certification in a language, such as C++ or Java. College graduates changing careers may return to a two-year community college or technical school for additional training. With expansion of intranets, extranets, and Internet applications, demand will increase for programmers with strong specialization in areas such as multimedia technology, client-server programming, and graphic user interface. Strong technical and communication skills are needed, with the ability to think logically and do analytical work accurately under pressure. Ingenuity, imagination, patience, and persistence are required to devise and apply programs.

Salary Range: $57,590 to $59,894.

☞ *Inside Track:* Employment prospects are best for college graduates with knowledge of a variety of programming languages and tools. Less formal education or its equivalent in work experience face strong job competition. Programmers are employed in nearly every industry, with a large concentration in firms that include software developers, telecommunications providers, financial institutions, insurance carriers, and government agencies. A large number of computer programmers are employed on a temporary or contract basis or work as independent contractors. Employment of programmers is expected to grow at a slower rate than that of other computer specialists due to prepackaged software and advanced technology. Employers, though, will continue to seek programmers with strong technical skills and who understand an employer's business. As employers enforce cost-control measures while trying to keep up with technology, programmers will be needed to assist in conversions to new computer languages and systems.

COMPUTER SUPPORT SPECIALISTS AND SYSTEMS ADMINISTRATORS

Job Skills and Requirements: Computer support specialists, or help-desk technicians, are troubleshooters who interpret problems and provide technical support for hardware, software, and systems. Systems administrators design, install, and support an organization's local area network (LAN), wide area network (WAN), Internet, or intranet systems. Bachelor's degree in computer science or information systems is preferred, but some employers may require only a computer-related associate degree or technical certification. With technical troubleshooting and customer interaction central to the job, solid problem-solving, analytical, and communications skills are necessary.

You must be a good listener to learn customers' problems, then patiently walk them through corrective steps. Strong writing skills are also helpful when preparing manuals for employees and customers. Keeping technical skills current and gaining new skills are critical to remaining marketable.

Salary Ranges: Computer support specialists $36,460 to $37,918. Systems administrators $51,280 to $53,331.

☞ *Inside Track:* Support specialists and systems administrators are projected to be among the fastest growing jobs, with the most openings through 2010. Job prospects will be best for college graduates who possess the latest skills and technologies. Certifications and related experience are essential for people without degrees. Employers will continue to seek specialists and administrators who have strong background in fundamental computer skills combined with good interpersonal and communications skills. With the continued development of the Internet, telecommunications, and e-mail, all types of businesses need specialists and administrators to develop and expand systems. Specialists and administrators may work either within a company that uses computer systems or directly for a computer hardware or software vendor. Increasingly, help-desk technicians work for help-desk or support service firms that clients contact.

DATA ENTRY AND INFORMATION PROCESSING WORKERS

Job Skills and Requirements: Data entry and information-processing workers type text, enter data, operate office machines, and perform other clerical duties using technology-based systems. High school diploma with word processing or data entry training and experience are preferred. Good spelling, punctuation, and grammar skills are essential, as well as general knowledge of standard office equipment and procedures. Employers generally hire those who meet their specific requirements for keyboarding speed.

Salary Range: $24,710 to $25,698.

☞ *Inside Track:* The need to replace workers who leave data entry and information-processing jobs each year will produce many job openings, and people with expertise in basic computer software applications will have the best job opportunities. Candidates can acquire skills in keyboarding and software, such as word processing and spreadsheets, through high schools, community colleges, business schools, temporary help agencies, or self-teaching aids such as books, tapes, and Internet tutorials. Large companies and government agencies typically have training programs to help administrative employees upgrade their skills and advance to other positions. These workers must continually upgrade skills to remain marketable.

DESKTOP PUBLISHERS

Job Skills and Requirements: Using computer software, desktop publishers format and combine text, numerical data, photographs, and other visual graphic elements to produce publication-ready material. Most workers qualify for jobs by taking classes or completing certificate programs at vocational schools, universities, and colleges. Although formal training is not always required, you will have the best job opportunities with certification or a degree, such as an associate's degree in applied science or a bachelor's degree in graphic arts, graphic communications, or graphic design. Because most materials are published on the Internet, electronic publishing skills, such as HTML, will provide an edge. Essential to the job are basic computer skills, a strong work ethic, and good communication skills. Artistic ability and good writing and editing skills are also helpful. Must be detail-oriented, work well independently, and have good visual abilities, including depth perception and color vision.

Salary Range: $30,600 to $31,824.

☞ *Inside Track:* Desktop publishers rank among the 10 fastest growing occupations, as more page layout and design work is performed in-house using computers and publishing software. Many new jobs are in firms that handle commercial or corporate printing and in newspaper plants; however, more and more companies in all types of industries are using in-house desktop publishers as a cost-saving measure. Most employers prefer to hire experienced desktop publishers, and job competition is expected to increase. For people without work experience, opportunities will be best for those having a computer background combined with certification or training in desktop publishing or graphic design. Job opportunities may be best in large, metropolitan cities.

Drafters

Job Skills and Requirements: Drafters prepare technical drawings and plans used by production and construction workers to build everything from manufactured products to structures, such as houses and gas pipelines. Completion of post-secondary school training in drafting is preferred. Candidates must have well-developed drafting and mechanical drawing skills, as well as knowledge of drafting standards, mathematics, science, and engineering technology. Problem-solving, artistic, and communication skills are critical, along with a solid background in computer-aided drafting and design techniques. Drafters must be detail-oriented and work accurately and neatly. Mechanical ability and visual aptitude are important as well as ability to draw three-dimensional objects both on computer and freehand.

Salary Range: $35,214 to $36,608.

☞ *Inside Track:* Job opportunities are best for people who have at least two years of postsecondary training in drafting and experience in using computer-aided drafting (CAD) systems. Employers seek drafters with a strong background in the fundamentals of drafting principles, a high level of technical sophistication, and the ability to apply knowledge to a range of responsibilities. Jobs remain highly concentrated in industries that are sensitive to cyclical changes in the economy, such as engineering and architecture. During recessions, drafters may be laid off, but a growing number of drafters are expected to be employed on a temporary or contract basis as more companies outsource their needs. People planning careers in drafting should take courses in math, science, computer technology, and computer graphics. Technical training obtained in the Armed Forces also can be applied to civilian drafting jobs, although some additional training may be necessary depending on the technical area.

ENGINEERS

Job Skills and Requirements: Engineers apply the theories and principles of science and mathematics to research and develop solutions to technical problems. Engineers have specialties that include electrical, chemical, civil, environmental, aerospace, biomedical, industrial, mechanical, nuclear, and petroleum engineering. Bachelor's degree in engineering is required for most entry-level jobs, with flexibility to work in different engineering specialties. Graduate degree is essential for engineering faculty positions and research and development jobs. All 50 U.S. states typically require engineers working with the public to be licensed as professional engineers (PE). Several states have imposed mandatory continuing education requirements for relicensure. Engineers must be creative, inquisitive, analytical, and detail-oriented. Good communication skills are important as engineers increasingly interact with specialists outside the industry.

Salary Ranges: Based on specialty.
>   Electrical engineer $64,910 to $67,506.
>   Engineering managers $84,070 to $87,433.

☞ *Inside Track:* Advancing technology will drive employers to seek qualified engineers to develop, improve, and update product designs and manufacturing processes. Engineering is one of the highest-paying occupations, with salaries ranging by specialty. Employment projections are good, but opportunities may vary by specialty. Engineering managers are among the fastest-growing occupations through 2008 as companies seek supervisors with advanced technical knowledge and strong communication and administrative skills. Many engineering jobs are related to developing technologies used in national defense. Throughout their careers, it is critical for engineers to continue their educations to stay on top of advancing technologies and to remain valuable to employers; however, even those who continue their education are vulnerable to layoffs if the particular technology or product in which they have specialized becomes obsolete.

SEMICONDUCTOR PROCESSORS

Job Skills and Requirements: Semiconductor processors manufacture semiconductors, or computer chips, using photolithography, a printing process for creating plates from photographic images. Associate degree in semiconductor processing or electronics technology is preferred. Hands-on training, or internships, while attending school will give job hunters an edge. Strong knowledge of mathematics and physical sciences is essential to advance in industry. Analytical, critical, problem-solving, and communication skills are important, as workers must anticipate problems and convey ideas both orally and in writing.

Salary Range: $25,438 to $26,457.

☞ *Inside Track:* Between 2000 and 2010, employment of semiconductor processors is projected to increase faster than the average for all occupations. Growing demand spurred from evolving technology and the need for chips in computers, appliances, machinery, vehicles, cell phones, and other telecommunications devices. Job prospects are best for people with postsecondary education in electronics or semiconductor technology. Semiconductor plants take careful measures to minimize contamination, with employees typically wearing special garments and working in environment-controlled rooms. Plants often operate around the clock, so it is common to work nights and weekends. Workers operate automated equipment and may spend a great deal of time standing at workstations.

Almost one-fourth of all electronic semiconductor processors belong to a union.

SYSTEMS ANALYSTS, COMPUTER SCIENTISTS, AND DATABASE ADMINISTRATORS

Job Skills and Requirements: Systems analysts, computer scientists, and database administrators encompass a broad range of computer specialists, including network systems analysts, Internet developers, and Webmasters, that require highly trained workers to design and develop new hardware and software systems and incorporate new technologies. Bachelor's degree in computer science, information science, or management information systems is essential, although some jobs may require only a two-year degree. Computer and information scientists typically require a doctoral degree due to the highly technical nature of their work, and companies increasingly seek graduate degrees for more complex positions. Must be detail-oriented and have strong logic, analytical, and technical skills. Ability to juggle several projects, work well with teams, and communicate effectively is important.

Salary Range: Systems analysts $59,330 to $61,703.
Computer scientists $70,590 to $73,414.
Database administrators $51,990 to $54,070.

🖘 *Inside Track:* These jobs are among the fastest growing occupations, with prospects in most industries, including government, computer, and data processing services and corporations. A growing number of computer specialists are employed on a temporary or contract basis—either self-employed or working for consulting firms. Many job openings will arise annually from the need to replace workers who move into managerial jobs or other occupations. Firms will continue to demand computer specialists who are knowledgeable about the latest technologies and who are able to efficiently implement them to meet business needs. The Internet and e-commerce are fueling demand for specialists who are knowledgeable about developing and supporting network, data, Internet, and intranet applications and, increasingly, computer security. Employers continue to seek computer specialists who have a strong combination of technical, interpersonal, and business skills and who can apply skills to help organizations use technology to communicate with employees, clients, and consumers.

chapter 10

THE PROFESSIONAL EDGE AND MORE: THE BEST PROFESSIONAL JOBS AND MORE

BUSINESS AND FINANCIAL SERVICES

Accountants and Auditors
Bill and Account Collectors
Budget Analysts
Claims Adjusters, Appraisers, Examiners, and Investigators
Court Reporters
Economists and Market and Survey Researchers
Financial Analysts and Personal Financial Advisors
Financial Managers
Lawyers
Paralegals and Legal Assistants
Property, Real Estate, and Community Association
    Managers
Securities, Commodities, and Financial Services Sales Agents

The material in this chapter comes from the Bureau of Labor Statistics (U.S. Department of Labor's *Occupational Outlook Handbook* and America's CareerInfoNet).

ACCOUNTANTS AND AUDITORS

Job Skills and Requirements: Accountants and auditors prepare, analyze, and verify financial documents for clients. Most jobs require a bachelor's degree in accounting, but some employers prefer a master's degree in accounting or business administration. Experience and professional certification or licensure will give an edge in the job market. Good computer skills are essential, as the job requires heavy use of financial software. Accountants and auditors need strong mathematical and analytical skills, as well as good communication skills to work with clients. Integrity is critical.

Salary Range: $43,500 to $45,240.

☞ *Inside Track:* Job growth will stem from increasing international business and mergers and acquisitions and from new companies requiring accountants and auditors to set up books, prepare taxes, and provide management advice. Competition is tough for jobs in major accounting and business firms, but the outlook is best for job seekers with certification or licensure and previous experience. The majority of U.S. states require Certified Public Accountant (CPA) candidates to be college graduates, and all CPAs must have a certificate. Prospective accountants and auditors should carefully research the licensure requirements of the state where they want to work. Increasingly, accountants will play more financial advisory roles in firms, and internal auditors will be needed to eliminate waste and fraud.

BILL AND ACCOUNT COLLECTORS

Job Skills and Requirements: Collectors keep track of overdue accounts and attempt to collect payment on them. High school diploma is required, but some employers may require college degree. Telemarketing or cash-handling experience helpful. Strong computer and financial software skills are important, and collectors must have good communication skills to work with people.

Salary Range: $25,314 to $26,327.

☞ *Inside Track:* With the continuing rise of consumer debt and with companies' increasing use of third-party collection agencies, bill and account collector employment is expected to grow faster than the average for all occupations through 2010. Hospitals and doctors' offices are two of the fastest-growing areas requiring collectors. Employment tends to rise during recessions. An employer may offer a candidate with a bachelor's degree a higher starting salary and more job advancement. Collectors typically receive on-the-job training in telephone techniques, negotiation skills, and laws governing debt collection. Collectors often work evenings and weekends and may spend a large part of the day on the telephone in a call center.

BUDGET ANALYSTS

Job Skills and Requirements: Budget analysts primarily provide advice and technical assistance in preparing annual budgets. Bachelor's degree is typically required, but some employers may require master's degree. Some firms prefer educational background in business, particularly statistics or accounting. May be helpful for candidates applying for government jobs to hold the Certified Government Financial Manager (CGFM) designation granted by the Association of Government Accountants. Strong mathematical, analytical, computer software, and communication skills are important, and budget analysts must be able to work well independently and under pressure.

Salary Range: $48,370 to $50,305.

☞ *Inside Track:* Job prospects are expected to grow, driven by the continuing demand for sound financial analysis in the public and private sectors. Job seekers with master's degrees and comfort with financial software packages will have the best opportunities. About two-fifths of all budget analyst jobs are with federal, state, and local governments, with the U.S.

Department of Defense employing 7 of every 10. Other major employers include schools, hospitals, and banks. Because financial and budget reports must be completed during periods of both economic growth and slowdowns, budget analysts typically are less subject to layoffs during economic downturns than other workers.

CLAIMS ADJUSTERS, APPRAISERS, EXAMINERS, AND INVESTIGATORS

Job Skills and Requirements: Adjusters, appraisers, and examiners investigate claims, negotiate settlements, and authorize payments, while investigators work with claims in which fraud or criminal activity is suspected. College graduates are preferred, with no specific major necessary. It is very helpful to have experience in a targeted profession to specialize in certain fields; for instance, college training in accounting will benefit adjusting financial loss claims, or an engineering degree will be helpful for adjusting industrial claims. Some states require licensure, so it is important to research state requirements. Must have good computer and analytical skills and must communicate effectively with claimants, witnesses, and other professionals. Continuing education is critical to keep current with new federal and state laws.

Salary Range: $41,080 to $42,723.

☞ *Inside Track:* Greatest demand for claims adjusters will be in health insurance and in property and casualty insurance. Investigator candidates will face tough competition from law enforcement and military retirees and other qualified experts. Working conditions for claims adjusters and appraisers typically include traveling to sites and inspecting automobiles and damaged buildings, which may provide potential physical hazards. Insurance investigators typically work long hours to conduct surveillance and to reach people evenings or weekends. Job may also involve stressful or dangerous confrontations with claimants and witnesses.

COURT REPORTERS

Job Skills and Requirements: Court reporters document with a stenotype machine reports of speeches, conversations, legal proceedings, meetings, and other events where written accounts are required. Two- or four-year postsecondary training program typically is required. The National Court Reporters Association (NCRA) has approved about 86 programs that offer courses in computer-aided transcription and real-time reporting. Some states may require a court reporter to be a notary public or a certified court reporter (CCR). Court reporters must possess excellent listening, grammar, and punctuation skills. To work in a courtroom, expert knowledge of legal terminology and criminal and appellate procedures is essential. Ability to meet deadlines and work under pressure also is required.

Salary Range: $39,660 to $41,246.

☞ *Inside Track:* Demand for real-time and broadcast captioning and accurate transcription of court proceedings will spur job growth for court reporters. Job seekers with certification from the NCRA will have competitive edge. The growing need to create television captions and provide the deaf and hard-of-hearing community with other real-time translating services, such as classroom translation, will create more job opportunities. The growing trend of conducting meetings and college classes via the Internet also will generate a need for court reporters to immediately deliver real-time transcripts.

ECONOMISTS AND MARKET AND SURVEY RESEARCHERS

Job Skills and Requirements: Economists research, collect, and analyze data, as well as monitor economic trends and develop forecasts. Market researchers analyze statistical data to predict future sales of products or services, and survey researchers design and conduct surveys to collect information. Employers typically require graduate-level degree for economist and market and survey research jobs. Entry-level economist positions in the federal government require bachelor's degree with a minimum of 21 semester hours of economics and three hours of statistics, accounting, or calculus. Research, analytical, quantitative, and computer skills are critical. Strong problem-solving and communication skills are needed. Must be detail-oriented to conduct precise data analysis, and must work well independently and with others.

Salary Ranges: Economists $64,830 to $67,423.
Market research analysts $51,190 to $53,238.
Survey researchers $26,200 to $27,248.

☞ *Inside Track:* Best opportunities will be for job candidates with graduate-level degrees and good communication skills. Additional skills in quantitative techniques that are applied to economic modeling and forecasting will provide competitive edge. To remain globally competitive, private industries are expected to hire more economists and researchers; however, state and local government job growth in this field is expected to slow. Employers seeking economists and researchers range from financial and health care institutions to manufacturing, market research, and advertising firms. Jobs typically are concentrated in large cities.

FINANCIAL ANALYSTS AND PERSONAL FINANCIAL ADVISORS

Job Skills and Requirements: Financial analysts and personal financial advisors research and analyze financial information and provide guidance to businesses or individuals. College education is required and master's degree in business administration is desirable. Studies in economics, statistics, and business are essential, and knowledge of accounting policies and procedures, corporate budgeting, and financial analysis methods is advantageous. Industry certification is not required, but recommended. Advisors who sell stocks, bonds, mutual funds, insurance, or real estate may need licenses to perform services. Must have good computer and financial software skills. Must be detail-oriented and self-disciplined and work well independently. Strong communication skills are critical to consult with clients and clearly present complex financial strategies.

Salary Ranges: Financial analysts $52,420 to $54,517.
　　　　　　　　Personal financial advisors $55,320 to $57,533.

☞ *Inside Track:* Demand for analysts and advisors will be spurred by individuals seeking more investment advice, financial services firms offering more investment-related services, and the globalization of the securities markets. Financial analysts will face stiffer competition for jobs at top securities firms. Most financial analysts work at large financial companies, many of which are based in New York City. Approximately one-fourth of personal financial advisors are self-employed who own and manage small investment advisory firms in urban areas. Sales and marketing skills are helpful to attract clients and build the necessary client base. It is essential to keep track of new regulations or policies that impact industry and to continually monitor the economy and its effect on clients' portfolios.

FINANCIAL MANAGERS

Job Skills and Requirements: Financial managers, including controllers, treasurers, and credit or cash managers, oversee the preparation of financial reports and strategies. Bachelor's degree in finance, accounting, economics, or business administration is required, but more employers are seeking master's degree in business administration, economics, finance, or risk management. Professional certification in specialized field is helpful. It is critical to have excellent interpersonal skills to manage staff and to effectively communicate complex financial data with others. Strong creative and problem-solving skills are helpful. It is important to have business operations knowledge and solid computer and financial software skills.

Salary Range: $67,020 to $69,700.

☞ *Inside Track:* Demand for sound financial expertise will create more opportunities. Job seekers with master's degrees and experience in accounting and finance will have an edge in marketplace. Candidates with risk management skills will be in great demand. The securities and commodities industry will hire more financial managers than other related industries. Many companies may temporarily hire financial managers for short-term projects. Continuing education will be critical to keep apprised of changing international, federal, and state regulations. Forecasting company earnings, profits, and costs and generating ways to increase profitability will become major role of corporate financial managers over the next decade.

LAWYERS

Job Skills and Requirements: Lawyers, or attorneys, perform advocacy and advisory roles. Bachelor's degree and law degree from school accredited by the American Bar Association (ABA) or proper state authorities are required. To practice law, you must pass state bar examination and be admitted to state bar. It is important to possess strong writing, speaking, reading, researching, and analyzing skills. Strong negotiating and reasoning skills are also essential. Lawyers practicing a specialty need solid background in that field; for example, tax attorneys must know accounting. It is important to work well with people as well as independently and to have solid computer skills to conduct legal research and produce documents. Lawyers must be willing to work long, hard hours and help build client base.

Salary Range: $88,280 to $91,811.

☞ *Inside Track:* Job outlook is strong with more legal action in such areas as health care, intellectual property, sexual harassment, environmental concerns, international matters, and elder care. Job competition will be stiff, though, with large number of law school graduates each year. Graduates with excellent academic records from well-respected law schools will have best opportunities. More employers will be seeking lawyers with experience in a specialty, such as tax or patent law. Lawyers will increasingly find jobs outside law firms, landing nonlegal positions complemented by a law degree, such as managerial roles in insurance firms, banks, real estate companies, and government agencies. Continuing education is essential to keep current with laws.

Paralegals and Legal Assistants

Job Skills and Requirements: Paralegals, or legal assistants, help lawyers prepare for closings, hearings, trials, and meetings. Graduates of postsecondary paralegal education programs or college graduates with paralegal certification are preferred. Graduation from a program approved by the American Bar Association is helpful. It is important to know litigation and general legal processes and to have a strong understanding of legal terminology and computer software. Excellent research and investigative skills are important, and paralegals must be able to effectively communicate in writing and orally to document and present findings. It is essential to complete work by deadline and to function well under extreme pressure.

Salary Range: $35,360 to $36,774.

☞ *Inside Track:* Strong employment growth is expected, as employers hire paralegals to lower internal costs and meet demands of workload. Job openings will stem from newly created jobs generated by rapid employment growth, with private law firms continuing to be the largest paralegal employer. Job opportunities are also expected to increase in the public sector, with consumer and community service organizations and government agencies hiring additional paralegals. Expect to face tough job competition as the number of graduates will outpace job openings.

PROPERTY, REAL ESTATE, AND COMMUNITY ASSOCIATION MANAGERS

Job Skills and Requirements: Property and real estate managers oversee the performance of commercial and residential properties and ensure that the properties meet expected revenues. Community association managers manage the property and services of condominiums, cooperatives, and other community housing through homeowners' or community associations. College graduates are preferred, with emphasis in business administration, accounting, finance, real estate, or public administration. Experience as a real estate sales agent is a plus. Managers of public housing subsidized by the federal government must be certified, and real estate managers who buy or sell property must be licensed in the state where they practice. Professional certification is helpful. Managers must understand and comply with local, state, and federal fair housing laws and building codes. Pleasant personality and excellent communication skills are required to effectively work with homeowners, residents, and other professionals. Must have strong computer skills and solid financial and negotiating abilities.

Salary Range: $36,020 to $37,460.

☞ *Inside Track:* Employment for real estate professionals is projected to increase faster than the average for all three occupations through 2010. Best opportunities will be for job seekers with college degrees in business administration or real estate and for those with professional certification. On-site property manager employment will be spurred by the growing number of apartments, condos, and offices and from more commercial and residential property owners using professionals to manage their investments. The aging population also will create more job opportunities for managers, with the expected rise of assisted-living facilities and retirement communities. Demand for property and real estate managers to operate these facilities will grow. As part of their compensation packages, many residential apartment and on-site association managers receive an apartment to live in, and managers employed in land development often receive a small percentage of ownership in the projects they develop.

SECURITIES, COMMODITIES, AND FINANCIAL SERVICES SALES AGENTS

Job Skills and Requirements: Investors use securities and commodities sales agents, or brokers, and financial services sales agents when buying or selling stocks, bonds, mutual funds, or other financial products. College degree is essential, and courses in business administration, economics, and finance are helpful. Some employers seek candidates with commission-based sales experience. Securities and commodities sales agents must meet state licensing requirements and must register with the National Association of Securities Dealers (NASD) as representatives of their firms. Solid knowledge in financial products, economic trends, and computer software is essential. Excellent sales and communication skills are critical.

Salary Range: $56,080 to $58,323.

☞ *Inside Track:* Job growth is expected to significantly increase as more people seek advice and services to reach their financial goals. Although Internet stock trading has reduced broker jobs for some transactions, the increased demand for advice and services will generate strong employment growth for agents. Seven out of 10 agents work for securities and commodities brokers, exchanges, and investment services companies, many of which are in New York City. Brokers who provide personalized service typically are paid commissions based on the amount of financial products they sell. Earnings typically fluctuate with stock market conditions, and most firms provide agents with a steady income by paying a minimum salary based on expected earnings. Financial services sales agents typically are paid a salary. All registered securities and commodities sales agents must attend continuing education classes periodically to maintain their licenses.

EDUCATION, GOVERNMENT, AND SOCIAL SERVICES

Arbitrators, Mediators, and Conciliators
Armed Forces
Child Care Workers
Correctional Officers
Counselors
Education Administrators
Instructional Coordinators
Librarians
Police and Detectives
Police, Fire, and Ambulance Dispatchers
Probation Officers and Correctional Treatment
     Specialists
Psychologists
Social and Human Service Assistants
Social Workers
Teacher Assistants
Teachers

ARBITRATORS, MEDIATORS, AND CONCILIATORS

Job Skills and Requirements: Arbitrators, mediators, and conciliators typically are attorneys or businesspeople who help opposing parties resolve disputes. Mediators who practice in state- or court-funded mediation programs must meet the training standards that particular state requires. Training is available through postsecondary schools and independent mediation programs and organizations. College degree is required, and it is helpful to specialize in public policy, law, or conflict management. Expertise in state and federal laws and in legal terminology is required. These professionals must possess strong conflict management and mediating abilities and have superior interpersonal communication skills to work with disputing parties. Adherence to the highest ethical standards is required.

Salary Range: $86,760 to $90,230.

☞ *Inside Track:* Employment is expected to grow as companies and individuals turn to arbitrators, mediators, and conciliators to avoid litigation, which can involve hefty fees, lengthy delays, and unwanted publicity. Arbitrators with expertise in the specific field in which they practice will have a competitive edge. The American Arbitration Association (AAA) requires mediators listed on its panel to complete an AAA training course, receive recommendations from trainers, and complete an apprenticeship. Arbitrators, mediators, and conciliators hold jobs mostly in state and local governments and in legal services.

ARMED FORCES

Job Skills and Requirements: Protecting the United States through a strong national defense involves a broad range of jobs, including managing hospitals, programming computers, repairing helicopters, and operating weapons. The military provides training and work experience for people serving in the Army, Navy, Marine Corps, Air Force, Coast Guard, and the Air and Army National Guard. Enlisted personnel, who comprise about 85 percent of the armed forces, perform military operations in areas that include combat, administration, construction, engineering, electronics, technical subjects, manufacturing, health care, and human services. Officers supervise and manage the military personnel in these various areas. High school diploma is typically required, and bachelor's degree or master's degree for specialty fields is needed for officers. To enlist, you must be between 17 and 35 years old, be a U.S. citizen or immigrant alien holding permanent resident status, and have no felony record. You must meet certain physical standards as to height, weight, vision, and overall health.

Salary Ranges: Military monthly pay varies by rank and total years of service. For enlisted personnel at lower grade levels with less than two years' experience, $1,043 to $1,085 monthly; for more than 20 years of service at higher grade levels, $11,049 to $11,491.

☞ *Inside Track:* Good job opportunities will exist in all branches of the Armed Forces. More than 365,000 enlisted personnel and officers must be recruited each year to replace those who complete their commitments or retire. Education requirements will continue to rise as some military jobs become more technical and complex. Carefully research all requirements for particular military branch of interest. It is highly recommended you learn about military life before making a commitment by talking with people who are holding roles of interest. On duty, many service people can gain college credit for technical training they receive. In addition to basic pay, military personnel receive free room and board or a tax-free housing and subsistence allowance, a military clothing allowance, medical and dental care, military supermarket and department store shopping privileges, and paid leave.

CHILD CARE WORKERS

Job Skills and Requirements: Child care workers teach and provide basic care for children of all ages in private households, child care centers, nursery schools, preschools, and other school-related programs. Training, qualifications, and licensing vary from state to state. High school diploma typically is required, but local governments, private firms, and publicly funded programs may have more training and education requirements. Workers must be constantly alert, anticipate and prevent problems, manage disruptive children, and provide fair discipline. They must communicate effectively with children and their parents. Maturity, creativity, and patience are required, as well as the ability to nurture and teach. Skills in music, art, drama, and storytelling are important.

Salary Range: $15,454 to $16,078.

☞ *Inside Track:* Good opportunities for qualified people will result from more families seeking alternative child care arrangements, high job turnover, and rise in the number of children enrolled in child care and preschool programs.

Working environment can vary from private homes and schools to child care centers and religious institutions. Work is never routine, and new challenges will arise each day. Child care can be physically and emotionally demanding, and hours may be long.

CORRECTIONAL OFFICERS

Job Skills and Requirements: Correctional officers maintain security—overseeing people convicted of crimes who are serving time in jails, reformatories, or penitentiaries, and overseeing people who have been arrested and are awaiting trial. Most institutions require applicants to have high school diplomas and no felony convictions. Job candidates typically are required to meet physical fitness standards. Federal, state, and some local corrections departments provide training, and many systems require firearms proficiency and self-defense skills. Officers must be in good health and able to respond quickly. Strong communication skills are essential to prepare reports on inmate conduct.

Salary Range: $31,170 to $32,417.

☞ *Inside Track:* One of the fastest growing occupations over the next decade, correctional officers will have excellent employment opportunities. Most officers work in large jails or state and federal prisons. Job growth will be spurred by rising inmate population, job turnover, and mandatory sentences requiring longer jail time, as well as expansion and new construction of facilities. Job can be extremely stressful and hazardous, as a number of correctional officers are injured in confrontations with inmates each year. Prison and jail security must be provided around the clock, so sometimes the job may require working nights, weekends, and holidays. Layoffs are rare because of growing inmate population.

COUNSELORS

Job Skills and Requirements: Counselors assist people with personal, marriage and family, educational, mental health, and career decisions and problems. Counselor jobs range from substance abuse to school or family. Bachelor's degree is required and master's degree is preferred, with studies in related counseling field. Most states require credentials, licensure, or certification. All states require school counselors to hold school counseling certification, with requirements varying by state. It is important to research education and training required by both counseling specialty and state and local governments. Strong desire to help people is essential, and crisis management and preventive counseling skills are important. Counselors must adhere to code of ethics. Excellent communication skills required to work effectively with people.

Salary Range: $42,110 to $43,794.

☞ *Inside Track:* Employment of counselors is expected to grow faster than the average for all occupations through 2010. Best opportunities will be for job seekers with master's degrees. Educational, vocational, and school counselor job growth is expected to rise due to increasing student enrollments and state legislation requiring counselors in elementary schools. There will be a strong demand for vocational counselors as people continually will seek career-related services, such as assistance switching careers, upgrading skills, or managing job hunts after layoffs. Substance abuse, rehabilitation, behavioral, mental health, and marriage and family counselors also will be in great demand as governments increase funds to improve services for children, adolescents, and families with serious emotional disturbances. Counselors must possess good physical and emotional stamina to manage working under stress and handle range of problems. They may work weekends and evenings to accommodate working people.

EDUCATION ADMINISTRATORS

Job Skills and Requirements: Education administrators, including supervisors, principals, and assistant principals, provide direction, leadership, and day-to-day management of educational activities in schools, businesses, and nonprofit and community

organizations. Most jobs require teaching or counseling experience and a master's degree or doctorate in education or related
field. Licensing requirements vary, depending on job and state.
Education administrators must have excellent communication
and business administration abilities and sound decision-making and organizational skills. Creativity is needed in developing innovative programs for quality education. Strong
computer skills and knowledge of latest educational tools and
computer-related software are essential.

Salary Range: $73,499 to $76,439.

☞ *Inside Track:* There is an excellent job outlook due to the
large number of administrators who are expected to retire
over the next 10 years and as enrollment of school-age children increases. More employment opportunities are projected in secondary and postsecondary schools, particularly
in rural and urban areas. Principals and assistant principals
will have best job prospects, as will college and university administrators seeking nonacademic positions, where there is
expected to be a deep shortage of qualified candidates. Most
education administrators work more than 40 hours a week,
and some work year-round. Some may find school over-
crowding, lack of teachers, and working with difficult students stressful and demanding.

INSTRUCTIONAL COORDINATORS

Job Skills and Requirements: Instructional coordinators, or curriculum or staff development specialists, develop instructional
materials, train teachers, and assess educational programs.
Bachelor's degree in education is important, but most employers prefer candidates with master's degree or doctorate in curriculum and instruction, educational technology, or related
field. Courses in curriculum development and evaluation, research design, and computers are recommended. Instructional
coordinators are required to keep skills current through continuing education. Excellent decision-making skills are necessary
to determine curriculum options, and strong communication,

administrative, organization, teaching, research, and computer technology skills are helpful.

Salary Range: $44,230 to $46,000.

☞ *Inside Track:* Demand for instructional coordinators will be generated from rising school enrollments and student services, as well as from greater emphasis on lifelong learning and on programs for students with special needs, including English as a Second Language (ESL). Coordinators will be instrumental in incorporating required government standards into the curricula and in developing new curricula to meet society's changing needs. They also will be needed to train teachers and to keep them apprised of new technologies and teaching techniques.

LIBRARIANS

Job Skills and Requirements: Librarians assist people in finding information and typically perform user, technical, and administrative services. Master's degree in library science (MLS) is required. For specialized libraries, such as medical and law libraries, it is advantageous to have coursework or degree in the related subject. Certification requirements for public school librarians vary from state to state. Solid Internet and computer research skills are critical, as well as capability to use numerous databases. It is important to continually stay on the cutting edge of computer technologies that impact the field. Strong communication, analytical, research, and organizational skills are required, and librarians must enjoy helping people.

Salary Range: $41,700 to $43,368.

☞ *Inside Track:* Job growth is expected stemming from retiring librarians, shortage of qualified candidates, and strong need for computer-literate skills. Job seekers with extremely strong Internet and computer skills will have competitive edge. Many companies will be seeking librarians because of their strong research, organizational, and information-management skills and their deep knowledge of computer databases. Good opportunities in nontraditional settings include law firms, corporations, information brokers, and consulting firms. Librarians also are hired by organizations to build and manage information for Internet sites.

POLICE AND DETECTIVES

Job Skills and Requirements: Police officers and detectives perform law enforcement duties to maintain law and order. High school diploma is required, but job requirements vary by community and agency. Bachelor's degree may be required for certain positions. It is helpful to take postsecondary school training in law enforcement-related subjects, including criminal justice and police science. Job candidates must be U.S. citizens, be at least 20 years old, and meet certain physical standards, with exams typically including vision, hearing, strength, and agility. Honesty, sound judgment, and integrity are critical. It is important to enjoy interacting with the public.

Salary Range: Police officers $39,790 to $41,382.
Detectives and criminal investigators $48,870 to $50,825.

☞ *Inside Track:* Employment of police and detectives is projected to increase faster than the average for all occupations through 2010, as people grow increasingly concerned with security and drug-related crimes. Opportunities will be best for job seekers with college training in police science or with military experience. More job opportunities are expected in local and special police departments, especially in urban areas. Work can be very dangerous and stressful. Officers must be constantly alert and prepared to deal with threatening situations.

POLICE, FIRE, AND AMBULANCE DISPATCHERS

Job Skills and Requirements: Police, fire, and ambulance dispatchers, or public safety dispatchers, are trained to handle calls from people needing emergency assistance and to initiate appropriate action. High school diploma is essential, and strong computer skills are required. It is critical to possess excellent communication skills and to work calmly under pressure. Basic office skills also are necessary, such as typing, filing, and record keeping. Residency in city or county of employment is frequently required. Some states may require certification to work on a state network, such as the Police Information Network.

Salary Range: $28,413 to $29,550.

☞ *Inside Track:* Increased demand for emergency services will spur employment growth for public safety dispatchers. Best opportunities will be for candidates with strong computer skills and experience or coursework in business, dispatching, or related fields. Working conditions may be stressful because of nature of phone calls, and job requires sitting for long periods of time using telephones, computers, and two-way radios. Recognizing the toll the job can have on workers, many employers will offer dispatchers training in stress and crisis management.

PROBATION OFFICERS AND CORRECTIONAL TREATMENT SPECIALISTS

Job Skills and Requirements: Probation officers supervise offenders on probation or parole through personal contact with individuals and their families. Correctional treatment specialists work in correctional institutions, such as jails and prisons, or in parole agencies. Educational requirements vary by state, but bachelor's degree in social work, criminal justice, or related field typically is required. Some employers may require master's degree. Most officers and specialists are required to complete training program sponsored by state or federal government, and some states may require certification. Strong knowledge of correctional laws and regulations is essential, as are strong computer and writing skills to prepare reports.

Salary Range: $38,150 to $39,676.

☞ *Inside Track:* Good employment opportunities are projected as a result of high crime rates and increasing prison, parole, and probation populations. The number of cases an officer or specialist handles depends on jurisdiction of agency and counseling needs of offenders. Officers may handle up to 300 cases at one time and must meet court-required deadlines; may be assigned to work in high-crime areas or institutions where there is risk of violence; may work with dangerous criminal offenders and interact with angry family members or friends; and may be required to carry a weapon. Although working under stressful conditions, many workers gain personal satisfaction from helping individuals become productive citizens.

PSYCHOLOGISTS

Job Skills and Requirements: Psychologists apply their knowledge to a range of areas, including health and human services, management, education, law, and sports. Clinical psychologists, who comprise the largest specialty, typically work in counseling centers, hospitals, clinics, or private practice. A doctorate degree is required for employment as a licensed clinical or counseling psychologist. Master's degree in psychology and related fields is necessary for other positions. Licensing requirements vary by state and by type of position. Psychologists must be emotionally stable, mature, caring, and able to effectively communicate and work with people. Patience, perseverance, and commitment to helping others are essential.

Salary Range: $48,320 to $50,253.

☞ *Inside Track:* Employment growth is expected stemming from increased health care needs in outpatient mental health and substance abuse treatment clinics, as well as in schools, social service agencies, and management consulting firms. Increased use of employee assistance programs by companies will also contribute to job growth. Best opportunities will be for people with doctorates in counseling, health, or educational psychology from leading universities. Applicants with extensive training in quantitative research methods and computer science will have competitive edge. Applicants with master's degree in school psychology will have best opportunities in schools. Those with only an undergraduate degree will have few career prospects.

SOCIAL AND HUMAN SERVICE ASSISTANTS

Job Skills and Requirements: Social and human service assistants have a range of job titles, including case management aide, social work assistant, mental health aide, and community outreach worker. High school diploma is required, but employers increasingly also seek people with postsecondary degree or certification in social work, human services, gerontology, or other behavioral science areas. Educational level often determines type of work and responsibility assigned. Good communication and time-management skills are essential. Social service assistants must be caring, understanding, and have a strong desire to help people.

Salary Range: $22,330 to $23,223.

☞ *Inside Track:* One of the fastest growing occupations over the next decade, social and human service assistant job opportunities are strong, particularly for people with postsecondary education. Demand will be spurred by replacing workers who advance to other positions or retire, as well as growing need for health care and elderly services. Good opportunities are expected in job-training programs, residential care facilities, and private social service agencies. Assistants will be needed to provide services to pregnant teenagers, substance abusers, homeless people, and mentally disabled and developmentally challenged people. Work can be rewarding, but emotionally draining. Understaffed programs and high turnover also may create work pressures.

SOCIAL WORKERS

Job Skills and Requirements: Social workers help people solve a range of personal problems. Bachelor's degree in social work, sociology, or psychology is essential, but many employers also require master's degree in social work or related field. All states have licensing, certification, or registration requirements. Excellent communication skills, high ethical standards, and sensitivity to cultural and diversity issues are essential. Social workers must be mature, responsible, and able to maintain good relationships with clients, as well as manage large case loads.

Salary Range: $31,470 to $32,729.

☞ *Inside Track:* Employment is projected to grow faster than average for all occupations through 2010 with increasing demand for health and social services, particularly in the areas of gerontology and mental health. As the population ages and the number of assisted-living and senior-living communities increases, candidates with background in gerontology will have excellent job opportunities. Employment also is projected to increase in hospitals and long-term care facilities in response to growing medical and social services needs. Volunteering and part-time jobs as a social work aide are ways to experience the field and see if you are interested in it as a career.

TEACHER ASSISTANTS

Job Skills and Requirements: Teacher assistants provide instructional and clerical support for classroom teachers, including tutoring students and helping prepare instructional materials. Educational requirements range from high school diploma to some college training. Employers increasingly prefer teacher assistants who have college training, and many schools require previous experience with children. Teacher assistants must enjoy working with children from diverse backgrounds, effectively manage classroom issues, and have thorough knowledge of instructional materials. Good record-keeping, computer, and audiovisual equipment skills are essential.

Salary Range: $17,350 to $18,044.

☞ *Inside Track:* Excellent job prospects are expected due to shortage of teachers spurring need for assistants to provide clerical assistance and classroom monitoring. Best opportunities will be in special education and English as a second language (ESL) classes. An increasing number of after-school and summer programs also will create opportunities. Assistants who speak a second language, particularly Spanish, are in great demand to communicate with the increasing number of students and parents whose first language is not English. Many assistants work toward a teaching degree while gaining experience. About 4 out of 10 teacher assistants belonged to unions in 2000, mainly the American Federation of Teachers and the National Education Association.

TEACHERS

Job Skills and Requirements: Teaching positions range from preschool to postsecondary and also include special education, adult literacy, remedial education, and self-enrichment. Education requirements and state certifications and licenses depend on type of teaching position. All states require public school teachers to be licensed. Teachers must have bachelor's degree and must have completed approved training program, as well as other testing requirements. Excellent reading, writing, and communication skills are critical. It is important to be dependable, patient, caring, and creative and to identify individual differences in students and help them achieve in school.

Salary Range: Elementary and secondary schools $37,610 to $39,114.

☞ *Inside Track:* Excellent job prospects are anticipated stemming from large number of teachers expected to retire over next 10 years and from shortage of qualified applicants. Elementary and secondary school teachers are among the occupations with the most job openings. Special education teachers and teachers with background in mathematics, science, foreign languages, and computer science will have good opportunities as a result of shortage of these specialties. English as a second language (ESL) teachers will have excellent job prospects as the immigrant population rises, as will self-enrichment teachers as more people seek lifelong learning to gain new skills and remain marketable in the workforce. Teachers who are willing to relocate to another city or state and who obtain a license in more than one subject will have competitive edge.

HEALTH CARE

Cardiology Technologists
Dental Assistants
Dental Hygienists
Emergency Medical Technicians and Paramedics
Medical Assistants
Medical Records and Health Information
    Technicians
Nuclear Medicine Technologists
Nursing and Home Health Aides
Occupational Therapist Assistants and Aides
Occupational Therapists
Pharmacists
Pharmacy Technicians
Physical Therapist Assistants and Aides
Physical Therapists
Physician Assistants
Radiologic Technologists and Technicians
Registered Nurses
Respiratory Therapists
Speech-Language Pathologists and Audiologists
Surgical Technologists and Technicians

CARDIOLOGY TECHNOLOGISTS

Job Skills and Requirements: Cardiology technologists operate cardiac-related medical equipment that helps physicians and other health practitioners diagnose and treat patients. High school diploma and training in two- to four-year accredited program are required. Graduates from programs accredited by the Joint Review Committee on Education in Cardiovascular Technology can receive professional certification through Cardiovascular Credentialing International in cardiac catheterization and other related procedures. It is essential to have pleasant personality and calm manner and to work well under pressure. Good organizational and record-keeping skills are required.

Salary Range: $33,350 to $34,684.

☞ *Inside Track:* As a result of the aging population, with older people historically experiencing heart-related problems, cardiology technologists will be in demand and are among the fastest growing occupations through 2010. The majority of jobs are in hospitals, and the work sometimes involves stressful life-and-death situations with patients. Some technologists may have to help doctors with routine office work and paperwork, including caring for equipment, scheduling appointments, and maintaining patient files.

DENTAL ASSISTANTS

Job Skills and Requirements: Dental assistants manage office and laboratory tasks, assist dentists, and provide patient care. High school diploma and training in accredited dental assistant program are required. Registration or licensing are also required in some states. High school or community college coursework in biology, chemistry, health, and office procedures is helpful. Good hand coordination is essential to handle sterile instruments. It is important to have a pleasant personality to deal with patients who are experiencing pain and discomfort. Being alert is vital, with a critical part of the job to protect patients and dental personnel from possible infectious diseases. A dental assistant must have the ability to take direction from the dentist and keep current with changing technology. Strong office skills also are important to schedule appointments and maintain patient records.

Salary Range: $25,979 to $27,018.

☞ *Inside Track:* Among the fastest growing occupations, dental assistants will be in greater demand as the population rises and aging people want to maintain their natural teeth and good oral hygiene. In addition, dentists seeking relief from heavy workloads will turn more to assistants to handle routine tasks. Higher education is required for job advancement, so many people work as assistants to gain experience in the field.

DENTAL HYGIENISTS

Job Skills and Requirements: Hygienists examine people's teeth and help patients maintain good oral health. Associate's degree is required to work in a private dental office, and bachelor's or master's degree is necessary for research, teaching, or practicing in public or school health programs. Degrees must be from accredited dental hygiene schools, determined by the Commission on Dental Accreditation. You must be licensed in the state where you practice and pass a written and clinical exam administered by the American Dental Association Joint Commission on National Dental Examinations. Most states also require an exam on legal aspects of the practice. With responsibility for protecting the health of patients and staff, it is critical to be proficient in radiological procedures and protective devices. Dental hygienists must work well with patients, be able to put them at ease, and have good manual dexterity to handle instruments.

Salary Range: $51,334 to $53,387.

☞ *Inside Track:* The demand for dental care, coupled with population growth, makes dental hygienists one of the fastest growing jobs over the next decade. Dentists will hire more hygienists to perform routine dental care, such as cleanings, so they can devote more time to other procedures. Dentists often hire hygienists to work only two or three days a week, so the flexible work schedule can be a very appealing aspect. With this flexibility, some hygienists hold jobs in more than one dental office.

EMERGENCY MEDICAL TECHNICIANS AND PARAMEDICS

Job Skills and Requirements: Emergency Medical Technicians (EMTs) and paramedics have training to perform prehospital medical procedures when dispatched to a scene by a 911 operator. High school diploma and training and certification required. Registration with the National Registry of Emergency Medical Technicians also is required at some or all levels of certification, depending on state requirements. EMTs must be technically trained in assessing patients' medical conditions and providing correct treatments under strict guidelines consistent with the level of training received. Computer technology is essential in assessing patient's condition, administering equipment, and applying life-support procedures. Paramedics must remain cool and calm under extreme pressure when seconds count. Good physical health and ability to cope with physical and emotional demands of the job are important. Excellent communication skills are essential in order to relay critical medical information to doctors and to interact with people in distress, as well as with fire, police, and other professionals.

Salary Range: $22,460 to $23,358.

☞ *Inside Track:* Job growth will be spurred by a rising population, particularly in urban areas, and the rising number of elderly people, who are more likely to have medical emergencies. Job seekers with advanced levels of certification will have competitive edge. Although job opportunities will grow in hospitals and private ambulatory services, competition will be greatest for jobs in police, fire, and rescue squad departments, where salaries and benefits typically are better. EMTs or paramedics who work in fire or police departments receive the same benefits as firefighters and police officers, which typically include pension plans that provide retirement at half pay after 20 or 25 years of service or if disabled in the line of duty. Job stress is common from irregular work hours and from treating people in life-or-death situations, but the work is challenging and rewarding.

MEDICAL ASSISTANTS

Job Skills and Requirements: Medical assistants perform administrative and clinical duties to ensure medical offices run smoothly. High school diploma is required, and it is helpful to have coursework in math, health, biology, and bookkeeping. Most employers prefer graduates of medical assistant programs accredited by the Commission on Accreditation of Allied Health Education Programs or the Accrediting Bureau of Health Education Schools. There is no licensing for medical assistants, but some states require a test or a course before assistants can perform certain tasks like taking X-rays. Medical assistants must be courteous, have a pleasant manner, and be able to put nervous patients at ease. Good communication skills are vital to explain doctor's instructions to patients. It is essential to have good computer and office skills.

Salary Range: $23,000 to $23,920.

☞ *Inside Track:* Employment growth will generate from group medical practices, clinics, and other health care facilities that need more support personnel to handle both administrative and clinical duties. Also, the aging population, booming health services industry, and medical advances will contribute to job growth. One of the fastest growing occupations, medical assistants will find more opportunities in outpatient settings. Job prospects are best for job seekers with formal training and experience. Volunteer work in the health care field also is helpful.

MEDICAL RECORDS AND HEALTH INFORMATION TECHNICIANS

Job Skills and Requirements: Medical records and health information technicians analyze the content of medical records, evaluate them for completeness and accuracy, and ensure proper information is recorded into the computer. Associate's degree from an accredited medical technician program is required, and it is helpful to have coursework in medical terminology, biology, statistics, database management, and health information law. Most employers prefer to hire Registered Health Information Technicians (RHITs) who were trained in a program accredited by the American Medical Association's Commission on Accreditation of Allied Health Education Programs. Excellent computer skills are required to use data analysis software, to complete computerized forms, and to manage volumes of medical records on databases. Good communication skills also are essential to interact with doctors.

Salary Range: $22,750 to $23,660.

☞ *Inside Track:* Among the fastest growing occupations through 2010, technician positions will rise as more clinics, group practices, physician offices, nursing homes, and home health agencies increase need for detailed records. In addition, as the number of medical tests, treatments, and procedures continues to rise, third-party payers, such as insurance companies, regulators, and consumers, will more carefully scrutinize medical records. Best job opportunities will be for candidates with strong clinical background. High school students can improve chances of getting into an accredited education program by taking anatomy, physiology, medical terminology, and computer courses.

NUCLEAR MEDICINE TECHNOLOGISTS

Job Skills and Requirements: Nuclear medicine technologists administer radiopharmaceuticals and operate sophisticated medical equipment to help doctors diagnose and treat patients. Certificate or associate's or bachelor's degree from nuclear medicine technology program at schools accredited by the Joint Review Committee on Education Programs in Nuclear Medicine Technology is required. Technologists must meet federal standards on administering radioactive drugs and operating equipment. It is important to be patient and detail-oriented and to possess good physical strength to lift or turn disabled patients. Solid mechanical and manual dexterity abilities are essential to operate complicated equipment.

Salary Range: $44,130 to $45,895.

☞ *Inside Track:* Job growth will be spurred by the increasing number of middle-aged and elderly people, the primary users of diagnostic procedures, who will face more medical problems with age and require nuclear medical tests. In addition, more technological advancements and wider use of nuclear medical imaging are expected to create more diagnostic uses for nuclear medicine. Most employers prefer applicants who earn a professional certification or registration from the American Registry of Radiologic Technologists or the Nuclear Medicine Technology Certification Board.

NURSING AND HOME HEALTH AIDES

Job Skills and Requirements: Nursing and home health aides help people who need routine health-related care or treatment. Nursing aides perform routine tasks under the supervision of nursing and medical staff. Home health aides assist elderly, convalescent, or disabled people in homes. Although no formal education is required, a high school diploma is helpful, and training or related work experience may be required by hospitals. Nursing homes typically hire inexperienced workers who must complete a minimum of 75 hours of training and pass a competency evaluation program within four months of employment. Aides who complete the program are certified and placed on the state registry of nursing aides. For home health aides whose employers receive Medicare reimbursement, federal law requires aides to pass a competency test. Aides must be in good health and be willing to perform repetitive, routine tasks. It is critical to be compassionate and caring and have a strong desire to work with people. Good communication and record-keeping skills are essential.

Salary Range: $18,491 to $19,230.

☞ *Inside Track:* Nursing and home health care aides will have great job prospects over the next decade, as the trend to cut health care costs will drive patients out of hospitals and nursing homes. Consumer preference for in-home care, the rising elderly population, and improved in-home medical technologies also will spur tremendous growth in this field. More emphasis on rehabilitation and long-term care needs of the aging population will increase demand for nursing aides. With a high turnover rate in this field, job opportunities for nursing and home health care aides will be excellent. The typically high turnover rate stems from low pay, lack of advancement, and physical and emotional toll, but work can be rewarding when helping patients in need.

OCCUPATIONAL THERAPIST ASSISTANTS AND AIDES

Job Skills and Requirements: Occupational therapist assistants and aides work under the direction of occupational therapists to provide rehabilitative services to people. Associate's degree or accredited certificate program is required for assistant jobs, and high school diploma required for occupational aides, who typically receive training on the job. It is helpful to have courses in biology and health and to have volunteer experience in nursing homes or occupational or physical therapist offices. Most states require assistants to pass a national certification exam. It is critical to be patient and caring and have strong communication skills to interact with patients and health care professionals.

Salary Range: $34,340 to $35,714.

☞ *Inside Track:* Occupational therapist assistants and aides, among the fastest growing jobs through 2010, will have good opportunities, resulting from an aging population expected to need therapeutic services. Medical advances and need to reduce health costs will generate a shift of hands-on therapy work from therapists to assistants and aides. Best opportunities will be for job seekers who have volunteer experience or who volunteer with the desired organization before applying for a job. Assistants and aides primarily work in hospitals, occupational therapist offices, and nursing and personal care facilities.

OCCUPATIONAL THERAPISTS

Job Skills and Requirements: Occupational therapists work with people who have mental, physical, developmental, or emotional disabilities to help them lead independent, productive lives. Bachelor's degree in occupational therapy from an accredited program and passing national certification exam are required. Occupational therapists must be licensed in states where they perform duties. It is helpful to have coursework in biology, chemistry, physics, health, art, and social sciences. Computer programming skills are necessary to help patients regain manual dexterity and thought processes on computer. Ability to work independently and good people skills are needed to help patients relearn skills. It is essential to be creative in planning therapies and activities; able to motivate patients and to use games, crafts, and other therapeutic tools; and strong for physically and emotionally demanding job. A patient, caring manner is critical, and good record-keeping skills are essential to maintain accurate medical records.

Salary Range: $49,450 to $51,428.

☞ *Inside Track:* Driving job growth for occupational therapists is the rapidly growing elderly population and the increasing number of middle-aged people, who statistically are more
vulnerable to heart disease and strokes. Therapeutic services
will be more in demand also at hospitals, which will need a
large number of therapists to provide therapy services to severely ill inpatients and to staff outpatient rehabilitation services. Schools will need therapists to serve disabled students.
Therapists are taking on more supervisory roles, and occupational therapist assistants and aides are performing more
hands-on tasks with patients, while therapists manage overall
activities. Job seekers with related volunteer work or experience will have competitive edge.

PHARMACISTS

Job Skills and Requirements: Pharmacists dispense prescribed
medications and provide information about their proper use.
Degree from accredited college of pharmacy is required, and
pharmacists must be state-licensed to practice. In addition to
degree, licensing includes serving an internship under a licensed pharmacist and passing a state exam. Excellent computer skills are essential to manage patient files, prescriptions,
inventory, and billing. Pharmacists must have high ethical
standards, be extremely accurate, and have great attention to
detail, as dispensing drugs can be a matter of life or death. A
strong desire to help others, great communication skills to interact with health care professionals and patients, and willing-
ness to work nontraditional hours are important.

Salary Range: $70,950 to $73,788.

☞ *Inside Track:* Contributing to the demand for pharmacists
are the expansion of retail and drugstores, a shortage of qualified candidates, and an aging population needing more medical attention. Opportunities also are growing for pharmacists
in managed-care organizations for research, disease management, and trend analysis in medication use. About 6 out of 10

pharmacists work in pharmacies that are part of a drugstore chain, grocery, or department store or are independently owned. Many of these pharmacies, as well as hospital pharmacies, are open 24 hours, so pharmacists may work evenings and holidays. Pharmacists' roles will expand to include drug therapy decision making and patient counseling. Continuing education is important to keep current with pharmaceutical advancements and treatments.

PHARMACY TECHNICIANS

Job Skills and Requirements: Pharmacy technicians help licensed pharmacists dispense medications to people. Degree or certification from pharmacy technician education program is essential. Classroom and laboratory work includes medical and pharmaceutical terminology, calculations, record keeping, law, and ethics. Strong math, spelling, and reading skills are critical, and a background in chemistry, English, and health education is helpful. Technicians must be fiercely detail-oriented and accurate and be able to take direction from pharmacists, as well as work independently. Strong customer service and computer skills are important. Excellent communication skills are required to interact with patients and health care professionals. Continuing education is important to keep current with new pharmacy-related technology.

Salary Range: $20,654 to $21,480.

☞ *Inside Track:* Good job opportunities are expected as retail pharmacies expand and as the pharmaceutical needs of the aging population increase. As insurance companies and health care systems seek ways to reduce costs, pharmacy technicians will assume more of the routine tasks previously performed by pharmacists. Job prospects will be best for technicians with formal training or previous experience, particularly those who have worked as aides in pharmacies or who have done hospital volunteer work. About two-thirds of technician jobs are in retail pharmacies, where responsibilities may depend on state regulations.

PHYSICAL THERAPIST ASSISTANTS AND AIDES

Job Skills and Requirements: Physical therapist assistants and aides, under supervision of physical therapists, help provide services to rehabilitate people with physical disabilities. High school diploma is required. Assistants must have associate's degree from an accredited physical therapist assistant program, and aides typically receive on-the-job training. Some states may have specific educational requirements and may require a license. Good communication skills are critical to work with patients and physical therapists. Workers must be able to take direction and have a strong desire to help people. Good physical strength is important to lift patients. Good record-keeping and computer skills are necessary to document patient progress and to fill out paperwork.

Salary Range: Assistants $33,870 to $35,225.
Aides $19,670 to $20,457.

☞ *Inside Track:* Physical therapist assistants and aides, two of the fastest growing occupations through 2010, will be needed to meet demand for rehabilitative services for middle-aged and elderly people who suffer chronic or debilitating conditions. Licensed assistants, particularly, will help health care facilities reduce costs as they, instead of higher-paid therapists, implement certain treatments. Most jobs are in hospitals or physical therapist offices, but many also work in nursing, home health, and outpatient rehabilitation centers.

PHYSICAL THERAPISTS

Job Skills and Requirements: Physical therapists help rehabilitate people with physical disabilities. Degree from accredited physical education program is required, and all states require therapists to be licensed. It is helpful to have coursework in biology, chemistry, math, anatomy, social science, and physics. Volunteer experience in a physical therapy department of a hospital or clinic may be required for some programs. It is critical to be compassionate, caring, and patient with people. Therapists must have good communication skills to interact with patients, their families, and doctors. Good physical strength is important to lift patients and move heavy equipment. Therapists must be able to use computer to program treatments and maintain patient records.

Salary Range: $54,810 to $57,002.

☞ *Inside Track:* Job opportunities are expected to be good with the aging population and the growing number of people with disabilities requiring long-term care and rehabilitation. More employers also are using physical therapists to evaluate work sites, where workers may be at risk to develop conditions like carpal tunnel syndrome, and to develop exercise programs. Medical advancements also will spur job growth as a higher percentage of trauma victims survive and need rehabilitative care. Most physical therapists work in hospitals or physical therapy offices, but jobs are expected to grow in home health agencies, outpatient rehabilitation centers, and doctors' offices.

PHYSICIAN ASSISTANTS

Job Skills and Requirements: Physician assistants perform diagnostic and therapeutic health care services under doctor supervision and in most states may prescribe medications. Degree from accredited education program is required, which typically involves two years of college and work experience in health care. Bachelor's or master's degree in health care field is preferred. Courses in biology, chemistry, math, social sciences, psychology, and English are helpful. After graduating from an accredited education program, a physician assistant must pass the Physician Assistants National Certifying Examination administered by the National Commission on Certification of Physician Assistants (NCCPA). Strong desire to help people and excellent communication skills are essential. Must be able to take direction from doctors and other health care professionals. Continuing education is critical to keep current with new medical technologies, procedures, and medicines.

Salary Range: $61,910 to $64,386.

☞ *Inside Track:* Among the fastest growing occupations, physician assistants will have good job opportunities as health care services expand and as insurance companies and health care facilities become more cost-conscious. Having assistants perform more primary care work and provide more assistance with medical and surgical procedures can significantly reduce costs. About half of assistant jobs have been in offices and clinics, but job prospects are projected to grow in hospitals, academic medical centers, public clinics, and prisons. More assistants also will be needed in teaching hospitals. Many job applicants are former emergency medical technicians or nurses, so bachelor's or master's degree in health care field will give competitive edge.

RADIOLOGIC TECHNOLOGISTS AND TECHNICIANS

Job Skills and Requirements: Radiologic technologists and technicians prepare and administer X-rays. High school diploma is required, and associate's degree from accredited training program is essential as well. It is helpful to have coursework in math, physics, chemistry, and biology. Many employers prefer to hire licensed radiographers. Registration in radiography is offered by the American Registry of Radiologic Technologists (ARRT). Bachelor's or master's degree in radiologic technologies is preferred for supervisory, administrative, or teaching positions. Strong communication skills and patience are important to interact with people, and good manual dexterity and mechanical ability are necessary to operate machines. Radiographers must accurately maintain patient records and must be able to strictly follow doctors' orders and government regulations regarding radiation use.

Salary Range: $36,000 to $37,440.

☞ *Inside Track:* Demand for radiologic technologists and technicians is generated from the shortage of qualified people. Strong job growth stems from the rising number of middle-aged and elderly people who will require medical care and diagnostic procedures. Job seekers with certification or degree in more than one type of diagnostic imaging technology, such as sonography or nuclear medicine, will have competitive edge and will be more attractive candidates for hospital positions. Jobs will typically be in hospitals, but opportunities are growing in clinics, doctors' offices, and outpatient facilities.

REGISTERED NURSES

Job Skills and Requirements: Registered nurses (RNs), including hospital, nursing home, public health, and home health nurses, provide patient care and assist physicians. All states require nurses to have degree from accredited nursing program and to be state licensed. Some employers require bachelor's degree for nursing administration jobs. Background in the sciences, humanities, and computers is important. Nurses must have good judgment, follow precise instructions, and be responsible, caring, and sensitive. Continuing education is critical to keep current with medical technologies and to renew license. Good record-keeping and administrative skills are important to maintain patient records.

Salary Range: $44,840 to $46,634.

☞ *Inside Track:* A shortage of qualified candidates, a rapidly aging population, and advancing technologies will spur job opportunities for registered nurses. This is the largest health care occupation, with more than 2 million jobs, and is one of the 10 occupations to have the largest number of new jobs. Most opportunities are expected in hospital outpatient facilities, including rehabilitation and chemotherapy centers. Nurses also will be needed for home health care and nursing homes, where there will be a great demand to serve the growing number of elderly requiring long-term care. Employment is also projected to grow in doctors' offices, clinics, and ambulatory surgicenters.

RESPIRATORY THERAPISTS

Job Skills and Requirements: Respiratory therapists administer respiratory care and life support to patients with heart and lung difficulties. Postsecondary degree is essential, and some states have licensing requirements. Coursework in health, biology, math, chemistry, and physics is helpful. Most employers require entry-level candidates to have a Certified Respiratory Therapist (CRT) credential, which is offered by the National Board for Respiratory Care (NBRC). Therapists must be sensitive, caring, and patient and have good communication skills. Good manual dexterity and mechanical abilities are essential to handle equipment.

Salary Range: $37,680 to $39,187.

☞ *Inside Track:* One of the fastest growing occupations over the next decade, respiratory therapists will be in great demand because of the increasing number of middle-aged and elderly people, who generally will be more susceptible to cardiopulmonary disease and respiratory ailments. Demand also will be spurred by advances in treating premature infants and heart attack and accident victims. Best opportunities will be for therapists with cardiopulmonary care skills or experience working with infants. Majority of jobs are in hospital respiratory, anesthesiology, or pulmonary departments, but increasing number of therapists will be needed in clinics, nursing homes, and home health agencies.

SPEECH-LANGUAGE PATHOLOGISTS AND AUDIOLOGISTS

Job Skills and Requirements: Speech-language pathologists work with people who have speech and language disorders, and audiologists work with people who have hearing, balance, and other related problems. Master's degree, 300 to 375 hours of supervised clinical experience, and nine months of postgraduate clinical experience are required by most states. Most states also require continuing education for license renewal. Background in anatomy, acoustics, physiology, science, math, and the mechanics of speech and hearing is helpful. Excellent communication skills are required to interact with patients. It is important to be patient, compassionate, and committed to helping patients.

Salary Range: $46,640 to $48,506.

☞ *Inside Track:* As one of the fastest growing occupations through 2010, pathologists and audiologists will be needed to meet the demand generating from the aging population who are more prone to hearing loss and to speech and language problems from strokes or other illnesses. Also spurring job growth are advances in treating premature babies and trauma and stroke victims. Job opportunities will increase in elementary and secondary schools, where enrollment continues to rise, and more pathologists and audiologists will be needed for special education services and for early detection and diagnosis of disorders. Speech-language pathologists typically work in schools, and audiologists are more likely to work in health care offices. With the rapid rise of outpatient care, professionals increasingly will go into private practice to contract work with hospitals, schools, and nursing homes.

SURGICAL TECHNOLOGISTS AND TECHNICIANS

Job Skills and Requirements: Surgical technologists, or scrub nurses, assist doctors with surgical procedures. High school diploma and formal training through accredited program are required. Employers prefer graduates with additional certification, which can be obtained through the Liaison Council on Certification for the Surgical Technologist. Coursework in health, biology, chemistry, and math is helpful. Agility is essential to manage various-sized instruments, and scrubs must have flexibility to respond quickly to doctors' instructions and to emergency situations. Ability to handle stressful operating room environment is critical.

Salary Range: $29,020 to $30,181.

☞ *Inside Track:* The rise in medical problems and procedures correlating with the rapidly aging population will create great job opportunities for surgical technologists, one of the fastest growing occupations over the next decade. Significant medical advances, such as laser technology, are also contributing to the projected rise in surgical procedures. Most job opportunities will be in hospitals, but there also will be more opportunities in doctors' offices, clinics, and ambulatory surgical centers.

HOSPITALITY

Chefs, Cooks, and Food Preparation Workers
Food and Beverage Servers and Related Workers
Food Service Managers
Gaming Services Workers
Hotel, Motel, and Resort Desk Clerks
Recreation and Fitness Workers

CHEFS, COOKS, AND FOOD PREPARATION WORKERS

Job Skills and Requirements: Chefs and cooks prepare meals, while food preparation workers assist. No educational or training requirements for entry-level food preparation position are needed, only basic skills of handling, preparing, and presenting food. For chefs, on-the-job training and courses in culinary arts at trade, vocational, and community colleges are required. For jobs in upscale restaurants, chefs must have training by a prestigious culinary school. Certification is important for high-level cooks and chefs. The American Culinary Federation offers courses for certification in specific categories, such as pastry chef, culinary educator, and executive chef. Most states require food workers to have a health certificate and knowledge of hygiene and sanitation. They must be able to work with a team, have good personal cleanliness, and possess an acute sense of taste and smell. Computer literacy is necessary for ordering and inventory.

Salary Ranges: Chefs and cooks $25,106 to $26,110.
Food preparation workers $15,350 to $15,964.

☞ *Inside Track:* Chefs, cooks, and food preparation workers are in great demand, stemming from substantial turnover and from the increasing size of the population, higher disposable incomes, and more leisure time for older people. Highly skilled chefs or cooks will have excellent job prospects as more people dine out and choose full-service restaurants with varied menus. Job growth will also be in educational and health service industries, including hospitals, nursing homes, and high schools. Some employers provide staff with uniforms and free meals; however, federal law allows employers to deduct from their employees' wages the cost or fair value of any meals or lodging provided. In some hotels and restaurants, kitchen workers belong to unions, including the Hotel Employees and Restaurant Employees International Union and the Service Employees International Union.

FOOD AND BEVERAGE SERVERS AND RELATED WORKERS

Job Skills and Requirements: Food and beverage workers, including waiters and waitresses, bartenders, and hosts and hostesses, provide customers with service in restaurants, bars, and other dining establishments. There are no educational requirements, but some employers may prefer to hire high school graduates. For bartenders, training at a vocational or technical school is helpful, and they must have knowledge of laws concerning sale of alcoholic beverages to customers. Good arithmetic skills are critical to total bills. Excellent customer service skills and a pleasant personality are essential. Servers must enjoy dealing with people and have a neat, clean appearance and good hygiene. A good memory and solid organizational skills are essential to keep orders straight and to recall names and faces of repeat customers.

Salary Ranges: Waiters and waitresses $13,354 to $13,888, excluding tips.

Bartenders $14,269 to $14,840, excluding tips.

Hosts and hostesses $14,456 to $15,034.

☞ *Inside Track:* Jobs will be plentiful for food and beverage servers and related positions, resulting from a high industry turnover rate and from people spending more money on leisure activities and increasingly opting to dine out. In more upscale restaurants and hotels, candidates with previous experience and some education will have advantage. In restaurants specializing in foreign foods, candidates fluent in that particular foreign language will have competitive edge. Tips comprise a major portion of earnings. In some establishments workers contribute a portion of their tips to a tip pool, which is divvied up and distributed to other staff. In some large restaurants and hotels, workers belong to unions, including the Hotel Employees and Restaurant Employees International Union and the Service Employees International Union.

FOOD SERVICE MANAGERS

Job Skills and Requirements: Food service managers direct the activities of businesses that provide food-related services to customers. Degree from two- to four-year hospitality management program is required, and bachelor's degree in restaurant and food service management is preferred. Professional certification as a Food Service Management Professional (FMP) is helpful. Solid leadership, customer service, and organizational skills are essential to manage daily business activities, including placing orders with suppliers and maintaining high-quality food preparation standards. Must be detail-oriented, be a good problem solver, and be a good team builder. Excellent communication skills are required to deal with customers, suppliers, and staff. Good computer and Internet skills are important to perform many tasks, including finding recipes, recruiting staff, and purchasing supplies.

Salary Range: $31,720 to $32,988.

☞ *Inside Track:* With more people dining out and the number of food establishments increasing, food service managers will have good job prospects through 2010. Jobs will grow in eating and dining places, and will significantly increase in educational and health care institutions, including hospitals, nursing homes, and assisted-living facilities. Job seekers with bachelor's or associate's degree in restaurant and institutional food service management will have best advantage.

GAMING SERVICES WORKERS

Job Skills and Requirements: Gaming workers, including dealers and slot machine attendants and technicians, work in casinos. High school diploma is preferred, and workers must have license issued by a regulatory agency, such as a casino control board or commission. Regulatory and age requirements vary by state, and a gaming worker must be a resident of the state where employed. Some casinos may require certification in gaming depending on position, and for supervisory level may require bachelor's or master's degree in hospitality or hotel management. The Atlantic Cape Community College's Casino Career Institute, for example, offers training in games, supervisory programs, machine repair, and surveillance and security. Most casinos also provide some in-house training. Superior customer service and communication skills are critical, and gaming workers must have flexibility to work in fast-paced, high-stakes environment. Pleasant personality and patience are essential to deal with irate customers. Integrity and honesty are critical in handling large sums of money.

Salary Ranges: Dealers $13,330 to $13,863.
Slot attendants $21,620 to $22,485.
Gaming supervisors $37,900 to $39,416.

☞ *Inside Track:* The significant rise in gaming, a multibillion-dollar industry, is generating job growth in this field. Increasing demand for additional table games in gaming establishments is also spurring job growth, particularly for gaming dealers. Best opportunities will be for job seekers with degrees or certificates in gaming or hospitality-related fields and with previous experience and strong customer service skills. Job growth will be expanding in established gaming states, including Nevada and New Jersey. In addition, more states will legalize gaming and launch new gaming establishments, including hotel and riverboat casinos.

HOTEL, MOTEL, AND RESORT DESK CLERKS

Job Skills and Requirements: Hotel, motel, and resort desk clerks perform a variety of services for guests. High school diploma is required. Lodging establishments typically provide on-the-job training, but additional coursework in lodging management is helpful for advancement. It is critical to have a pleasant personality and excellent customer service and communication skills to interact with guests. Fluency in English, a clear speaking voice, and good computer skills are important. Neat and clean appearance is essential.

Salary Range: $16,380 to $17,035.

☞ *Inside Track:* Increased leisure travel and demand for extended-stay lodging will generate employment growth in the industry. In addition, more hotels and motels are being built to meet growing demand. Job opportunities will be best for those with excellent interpersonal skills and pleasant personalities. Fluency in a foreign language is helpful. Must have flexibility to manage variety of responsibilities, including checking in guests, answering phones, and problem solving.

RECREATION AND FITNESS WORKERS

Job Skills and Requirements: Recreation and fitness workers, including recreation leaders, aerobics instructors, and fitness trainers, plan, organize, and direct various leisure-time activities, such as aerobics, arts and crafts, dance, swimming, or tennis classes. High school diploma is mandatory. Some employers may require associate's or bachelor's degree in health and fitness, physical education, parks and recreation, social work, or leisure studies. Bachelor's degree and experience are preferred for administrative or supervisory positions. Specialized training or experience in a particular activity, such as swimming, music, or art, is helpful. Certification may be required for specific jobs, such as swimming coach or personal trainer. Some employers also require certification in first aid. It is important to be a good motivator and have good mentoring and coaching skills. Outgoing personality and excellent physical health are essential.

Salary Range: $17,139 to $17,825.

☞ *Inside Track:* Job growth for recreation and fitness workers is increasing, as more people concentrate on personal health and fitness and spend more money on leisure-time activities. Opportunities are projected to be best for fitness trainers and aerobic instructors. A rising demand for recreational and fitness activities for older adults in senior centers and retirement communities also is spurring employment growth. In addition, more workers will be needed to develop and lead programs in halfway houses, children's homes, and day care programs for people with special needs. Job openings are also expected to increase in camps, sports clinics, athletic clubs, and amusement parks. Best opportunities are for candidates with formal training and experience gained in part-time or seasonal recreation jobs.

MANAGEMENT AND OFFICE PERSONNEL

Chief Information Officers
Customer Service Representatives
Human Resources, Training, and Labor Relations Managers and Specialists
Management Analysts
Security Guards and Gaming Surveillance Officers

CHIEF INFORMATION OFFICERS

Job Skills and Requirements: Chief Information Officers (CIOs) are senior management level executives responsible for the overall technological direction of organizations. Bachelor's degree is required and master's degree in business administration is preferred. CIOs must have excellent communication, leadership, and people skills. Sound business judgment and analytical and problem-solving skills are essential. Vision is important in order to stay ahead of competitors and to develop and execute business strategies. Must have solid administrative, management, and human resources skills for hiring, supervising, and mentoring employees and for overseeing budgets and company operations. To remain competitive, it is critical to keep current with evolving technologies and information management trends, especially as they relate to the industry in which the CIO works.

Salary Range: $61,160 to $63,606.

☞ *Inside Track:* With technology and information management rapidly changing, it has become even more critical for organizations to have superior technological systems and skilled employees in place to stay competitive. Vital to an organization's competitive edge is a savvy information technology leader. Chief Information Officer positions will continue growing to meet this need, particularly in the business services industry. Job openings also will be generated by executives transferring to other positions, retiring, or leaving to start their own businesses. Experienced managers with strong leadership qualities and proven track records in improving competitive position and operating efficiencies will have best opportunities.

CUSTOMER SERVICE REPRESENTATIVES

Job Skills and Requirements: Customer service representatives answer customers' questions about products and services and handle and resolve complaints. High school diploma is required. Company products and services knowledge, typically acquired on the job, is critical in order to accurately answer customer questions, resolve issues, and positively represent the business. Excellent communication, customer service, computer, and telephone skills are essential. Good spelling and typing skills are important in order to answer customer inquiries via e-mail and to maintain accurate customer records. A clear speaking voice and fluency in the English language are necessary, as well as a professional appearance and a pleasant personality.

Salary Range: $24,600 to $25,584.

☞ *Inside Track:* Job opportunities for customer service representatives are expected to increase significantly, resulting from the exploding use of web sites for commerce and for communicating with current and prospective customers. More representatives will be needed over the next decade to answer questions via e-mail, help customers navigate web sites, and explain details of products and services. Job seekers with pleasant personalities and strong communication and problem-solving skills will have edge.

HUMAN RESOURCES, TRAINING, AND LABOR RELATIONS MANAGERS AND SPECIALISTS

Job Skills and Requirements: Human resources workers, including recruiters, trainers, benefits specialists, and equal employment opportunity (EEO) officers, manage employers' personnel needs, including recruiting skilled staff and developing and coordinating personnel programs and policies. Bachelor's degree is required, and it is helpful to have coursework or major in human resources, personnel administration, or industrial and labor relations. Graduate degree in industrial relations is preferred for labor relations jobs, and law background is preferred for employee benefits managers and other roles that require interpreting changing workplace laws and regulations. Human resources workers must have excellent communication and people skills, and must have solid administrative and business abilities. Good conflict-management and advising skills are important. Knowledge of federal and state workplace laws is essential.

Salary Ranges: Human resources managers $59,000 to $61,360.
Training specialists $40,830 to $42,463.
Benefits specialists $41,660 to 43,326.

☞ *Inside Track:* Demand for human resources specialists will rise, as organizations increasingly need experts to manage legislative standards for workplaces, including occupational safety and health, family leave, fair wages, sexual harassment and discrimination issues, and equal opportunity. Rising health care costs and high employee turnover rates also will be contributing to a demand for specialists who can help organizations be more cost-efficient. Job growth will be strong in management, consulting, and staffing firms and in organizations that develop and administer employee benefits and compensation packages. Continuing education is important in order to keep apprised of industry trends and workplace laws and regulations.

MANAGEMENT ANALYSTS

Job Skills and Requirements: Management analysts, or consultants, propose ways to improve an organization's structure, efficiency, or profits. Most employers in the private sector typically seek people with master's degree in business administration, and some also require at least five years' experience in the field in which they plan to consult. For government agencies, a bachelor's degree is sufficient for entry-level jobs. Must be self-motivated and disciplined, with strong analytical, time-management and communication skills. Good judgment, creativity, and ability to work well with individuals and teams are important.

Salary Range: $55,040 to $57,242.

☞ *Inside Track:* Job prospects are projected to grow faster than average, as firms increasingly rely on management analysts to help them retain a competitive edge; however, job competition is fierce. Thirty-three percent of management analysts are self-employed consultants, and job opportunities are expected to be best for those with a graduate degree, knowledge of the related industry and of traditional business practices, technical expertise, and sales and public relations skills. Job growth is projected in very large consulting firms that specialize in specific areas, such as biotechnology, health care, information technology, telecommunications, and engineering. Self-employed consulting opportunities may be hindered by increasing use of reputable consulting firms to examine a variety of organizational issues. Firms expanding their businesses outside the United States also will drive demand for analysts to help strategize entry into new markets abroad. Work involves meeting tight deadlines and travel, and self-employed consultants must bear costs of running their own businesses. International work may require knowledge of foreign language.

SECURITY GUARDS AND GAMING SURVEILLANCE OFFICERS

Job Skills and Requirements: A new and expanding area is airport security. Security guards protect property, maintain security, and enforce regulations at organizations, and gaming surveillance officers observe casino operations for illegal activities, such as cheating or theft, by customers or employees. High school diploma is preferred for both armed and unarmed guards. For gaming surveillance officers, it is helpful to have previous security experience and professional certification. Most states require guards to be licensed, which involves classroom training in property rights, emergency procedures, and detention of suspected criminals. Armed guards must be licensed by appropriate government authority to carry weapon. Security workers must have good character references, no serious police record, and strong physical health. It is critical to have good judgment and keen observation skills and important to be alert, emotionally stable, and agile to adeptly handle emergencies. Computer literacy is necessary in order to work surveillance equipment. Good communication and record-keeping skills are essential to interview witnesses and carefully document events. For federal government jobs, security workers must have previous experience and qualify for firearm use, and must pass first-aid test and U.S. General Services Administration certification exam.

Salary Ranges: Security guards: $17,570 to $18,273.
Federal government guards $28,960 to $30,118.
Gaming surveillance officers $21,220 to $22,069.

Inside Track: Excellent job growth for security guards and gaming surveillance officers is projected through 2010, as concern for crime and vandalism is rising. Following the September 11 terrorist attacks, safety and security have become a top priority. With a heightened concern for security, more establishments will seek qualified guards and officers to protect people and property. Job growth in private security firms and contract agencies will increase as demand grows for guards to monitor crowds in airports and in other highly populated, public areas. With trend of building more casinos and with more states planning to legalize gambling, gaming surveillance officers will be in high demand in casinos.

MANUFACTURING, REPAIR, CONSTRUCTION, AND TRANSPORTATION

Automotive Service Technicians and Mechanics
Carpenters
Construction and Building Inspectors
Electricians
Hazardous Materials Removal Workers
Industrial Designers
Landscape Architects
Line Installers and Repairers
Medical Equipment Repairers

Production, Planning, and Expediting Clerks
Truck Drivers
Water and Liquid Waste Treatment Plant and
    System Operators

AUTOMOTIVE SERVICE TECHNICIANS AND MECHANICS

Job Skills and Requirements: Automotive service technicians and mechanics use technology to diagnose and fix automobiles and light trucks with problems. Degree in automotive service technician program from high school or postsecondary vocational school is required. Coursework in auto repair, English, math, electronics, physics, and computers is helpful. It is important also to be certified by the National Institute for Automotive Service Excellence (ASE), which establishes training standards. Good communication and customer service skills are essential when listening to customers describe car problems and in turn explaining to them what needs to be done. Auto repairers must have excellent problem-solving, analytical, and mechanical skills, and must know intricacies of cars or trucks. It is critical to have knowledge of electronics and computers, as automobile features operate from computer- or electronic-based systems. Continual education is necessary in order to stay on top of automotive technologies and diagnostic techniques.

Salary Range: $28,496 to $29,636.

☞ *Inside Track:* Skilled technicians and mechanics will be in demand over the next decade, as sophisticated technology in cars and light trucks generates need for highly trained experts. Strong job growth is expected in dealerships, independent automotive repair shops, and small retail operations that offer after-warranty repair. Best opportunities will be for job seekers who graduate from formal automotive technician training programs and who have good diagnostic and problem-solving skills. Some technicians are members of labor unions, such as the International Association of Machinists and Aerospace

Workers, United Automobile Workers, or the International Brotherhood of Teamsters.

CARPENTERS

Job Skills and Requirements: Carpenters perform a variety of construction activities to build structures such as buildings, bridges, and boats. High school diploma is preferred, with courses in carpentry, shop, mechanical drawing, and math. Carpenters typically learn the trade through on-the-job training or through vocational training programs. Most employers recommend learning the craft through an apprenticeship program, administered by local chapters of the Associated Builders and Contractors and the Associated General Contractors, as well as by the United Brotherhood of Carpenters and Joiners of America and the National Association of Home Builders. To join a program, apprentices must be 17 years old and meet local requirements. Doing carpentry requires manual dexterity, good eye-hand coordination, and knowledge of tools. Math skills and ability to read blueprints and mechanical drawings are essential.

Salary Range: $32,635 to $33,940.

☞ *Inside Track:* Job prospects will be excellent for carpenters through 2010, with boom in new construction of homes and commercial buildings and growing demand for home and commercial building renovation and remodeling. Best opportunities will be for carpenters with more than one specialty and who have overall training that allows them to switch from residential to commercial construction and from remodeling to renovating. Having well-rounded skills will help job seekers land a new project more easily when one project ends. About one-third of carpenters work for general building contractors, and 12 percent work in heavy construction. Some carpenters change employers each time they finish a construction job or alternate between working independently and working for a contractor.

CONSTRUCTION AND BUILDING INSPECTORS

Job Skills and Requirements: Construction and building inspectors examine the construction of buildings, highways, sewer and water systems, bridges, and other structures to ensure compliance with codes, ordinances, and regulations. High school diploma is required, and associate's degree from community college is preferred. Coursework in engineering, architecture, construction and building technology, drafting, and mathematics is helpful. An inspector may be required by local government to pass a civil service exam or obtain certification. It is essential to have experience as a construction manager, supervisor, or craftworker, or have experience as a carpenter, electrician, plumber, or pipe fitter. It is necessary to have strong technical skills and knowledge of construction materials and practices, including evaluating blueprints and plans. Continuing education is important in order to keep current with construction materials and techniques and to keep apprised of government code requirements.

Salary Range: $38,750 to $40,300.

☞ *Inside Track:* With the growing concern for public safety and the rising number of real estate transactions, inspectors will be in demand to ensure quality construction. More home inspections also are driving job growth. Job opportunities will be best for highly skilled and experienced inspectors who have some college education, formal training in engineering or architecture, or certification as construction inspectors or plan examiners. Most inspectors work for local government agencies, but job growth will rise in engineering and architectural services firms.

ELECTRICIANS

Job Skills and Requirements: Electricians maintain electrical systems in homes and buildings. High school diploma and four- or five-year apprenticeship program are required. Coursework in math, electricity, electronics, mechanical drawing, science, and shop provides good background. Apprenticeship programs are offered by several organizations, including the International Brotherhood of Electrical Workers, the National Electrical Contractors, the Associated Builders and Contractors, or the Independent Electrical Contractors Association. Licensing requirements vary by state, and electricians may be required to pass an examination. Good manual dexterity is important for working with tools and small wires, and good color vision is necessary to identify different colored electrical wires. It is necessary to have strong knowledge of electronics in order to work with complex electrical systems and equipment controls.

Salary Range: $40,123 to $41,728.

☞ *Inside Track:* With rise in new and rehab construction and in emerging technologies, job prospects will be excellent for electricians through 2010. Skilled technicians will be in demand to install electrical devices and wiring in homes and other structures and to prewire office buildings during construction for computer and telecommunications equipment. In addition, more factories will use robotic and other computer-based machinery, so electricians will be needed to install and maintain these systems. Many construction electricians are members of the International Brotherhood of Electrical Workers.

HAZARDOUS MATERIALS REMOVAL WORKERS

Job Skills and Requirements: Hazardous materials removal workers, including lead-abatement workers and decontamination technicians, identify, remove, package, transport, and dispose of hazardous materials such as asbestos, radioactive materials, and lead. High school diploma is required. Technical training typically is provided on the job, and a license to work as a hazardous materials removal worker is required. Some disciplines, including asbestos, lead, and nuclear hazard removal, require certification through formal training program. Employers prefer to hire workers licensed in multiple disciplines. These workers must be detail-oriented, dependable, and knowledgeable in construction practices. It is critical to follow closely strict directions in order to minimize danger. Discipline and the ability to work well in stressful environment associated with hazardous materials are essential.

Salary Range: $28,517 to $29,658.

☞ *Inside Track:* Increased public safety and health awareness and more federal and state regulations are generating high demand for trained workers to remove hazardous materials from the environment, public places, office buildings, homes, and other structures. In addition, there will be job growth stemming from pressure to have safer and cleaner nuclear and electrical generator facilities. Strong demand is projected over the next decade for lead-abatement workers and for decontamination technicians, radiation safety technicians, and decommissioning workers. Working conditions can be extremely difficult and stressful, and protective suits are worn for safety. Opportunities are best in private contractor firms.

INDUSTRIAL DESIGNERS

Job Skills and Requirements: Industrial designers develop manufactured products, including toys, cars, planes, computer equipment, medical equipment, and home appliances. Bachelor's degree in industrial design or fine arts is required, and master's degree will provide competitive edge. Background in art, market research, aesthetics, problem solving, manufacturing, and materials is helpful. Industrial designers must be highly skilled in using computer-aided design (CAD) software programs, and must have excellent freehand sketching skills. Must be able to communicate ideas effectively in speech, in writing, and visually. Creativity, imagination, strong sense of color and design, and a good eye for detail are important. It also is necessary to keep current with cultural trends.

Salary Range: $48,780 to $50,731.

☞ *Inside Track:* Job opportunities for industrial designers will be good over the next decade, benefiting from stronger emphasis on product quality and safety and on developing high-technology products in medicine and transportation. In addition, people increasingly want new, easy-to-use products, and companies increasingly need new concepts to remain globally competitive. Job seekers with master's degree, creative flair, and good business sense will have edge. Candidates with solid portfolios that reflect talent and skill and that include successful products will have advantage.

LANDSCAPE ARCHITECTS

Job Skills and Requirements: Landscape architects design residential areas, parks, campuses, shopping centers, and other locations for functionality, beauty, and compatibility with the natural environment. Bachelor's or master's degree in landscape architecture is required. Coursework in surveying, design, construction, ecology, plant and soil science, and urban and regional planning is helpful. Most states require license based on the Landscape Architect Registration Examination (LARE), and some may have additional registration requirements. It is essential to have strong love of nature and enjoy working with your hands. Creativity, artistic talent, and writing skills are important. Landscape architects must be skilled in computer-aided design (CAD) software programs and work well both with team members and independently.

Salary Range: $43,540 to $45,282.

☞ *Inside Track:* Strong growth in residential, commercial, and heavy construction will spur demand for landscape architects to design aesthetically pleasing areas. Increased emphasis on preservation and restoration of historic areas and wetlands, as well as emphasis on environmental safety and health, will also be generating good job opportunities for landscape architects. Job seekers who have strong computer design skills, good verbal and writing abilities, and strong knowledge of environmental codes and regulations will have edge. It is advantageous to have additional training or experience in urban planning when applying for jobs in landscape architecture firms that specialize in site planning.

LINE INSTALLERS AND REPAIRERS

Job Skills and Requirements: Line installers and repairers construct and maintain networks of wires and cables that provide customers with electrical power and communications services. High school diploma is required, and technical training in electronics and electricity from vocational school or community college is preferred. Basic knowledge of algebra and trigonometry, strong mechanical skills, and good physical strength to lift heavy objects and climb poles are all essential. Strong eye for color is important to distinguish color-coded wires and cables, and good communication and customer service skills are needed for working with customers.

Salary Range: $45,780 to $47,611.

☞ *Inside Track:* Generating job growth for installers and repairers is the booming telecommunications industry, which involves Internet, telephone, and cable television connective networks. Industry deregulation has spurred job opportunities, as companies increasingly are building new networks and offering more telecommunications services to customers, including high-speed Internet, digital cable, and multiple phone and fax lines. Companies also will upgrade existing systems to stay competitive. Rapidly evolving technologies will spur continued need for skilled workers to install and maintain next-generation data, video, and graphic networks. Best opportunities will be for candidates with strong skills and experience. Most workers belong to unions, among them, the Communications Workers of America.

MEDICAL EQUIPMENT REPAIRERS

Job Skills and Requirements: Medical equipment repairers work on mechanical systems that include electric wheelchairs, mechanical lifts, hospital beds, and customized vehicles. High school diploma is required, and skills are acquired mainly on the job. Background in electronics is helpful, as is specializing in equipment model and brand. Repairers must have good reading skills in order to understand technical manuals, and must have good vision. It is essential to enjoy problem solving, working with tools, and disassembling machines to see how they work.

Salary Range: $35,339 to $36,753.

☞ *Inside Track:* With significant increase in health care needs, medical equipment repairers will have good job prospects through 2010. The growing elderly population, who typically will require wheelchairs and other customized medical equipment, is also spurring job growth in this field. Medical equipment repairers typically work for hospitals or wholesale equipment suppliers.

PRODUCTION, PLANNING, AND EXPEDITING CLERKS

Job Skills and Requirements: Production, planning, and expediting clerks coordinate the flow of information, work, and materials to ensure production or shipment schedules are met on deadline. High school diploma is preferred, and production clerks must have basic knowledge of computers and basic office equipment. Typing, filing, record keeping, and other clerical skills are important, and excellent organizational skills are required to meet deadlines. It is important to know how company operates to efficiently schedule shipment of parts, staff workers, estimate costs, keep inventory, and assemble materials.

Salary Range: $30,597 to $31,820.

☞ *Inside Track:* With increased global business competition, companies need to produce and deliver products in a timely manner. This increased emphasis on speed and efficiency during the production process will spur demand for production, planning, and expediting clerks. Forty-four percent of all such jobs are in the manufacturing industry, and other jobs are in wholesale trade and groceries and the personnel supply services industry.

TRUCK DRIVERS

Job Skills and Requirements: Truck drivers travel short distances or across the nation's highways and interstates to deliver goods. All truck drivers must comply with strict state and federal truck-driving regulations and standards. A driver's license is issued by the state in which the driver lives, and a clean driving record is necessary. Some jobs may require a commercial driver's license (CDL), and there are very specific requirements for interstate truck driving. The U.S. Department of Transportation requires truck drivers in interstate commerce to be at least 21 years old, pass a physical exam, have good hearing, and have at least 20/40 vision with or without glasses. For some trucking firms, a driver must be at least 22 years old, have earned a high school diploma, and have had three to five years' experience. It is important to research state and federal requirements to obtain proper driver qualifications. Truck drivers must be able to keep good records, have physical and mental endurance, be courteous, remain constantly alert, and handle long, solo assignments. They must know the latest road safety procedures for protecting transported products.

Salary Range: $31,720 to $32,988.

☞ *Inside Track:* Job growth stemming from increasing use of rail, air, and ship transportation, which require trucks to pick up and deliver shipments, and from increasing need for drivers to transport perishable and time-sensitive goods. Truck driving has among the largest number of job openings each year, and the strong demand will create thousands more openings, particularly as experienced drivers retire or switch careers. Many truck drivers are members of the International Brotherhood of Teamsters.

WATER AND LIQUID WASTE TREATMENT PLANT AND SYSTEM OPERATORS

Job Skills and Requirements: Water treatment plant and system operators ensure water is safe to drink, and liquid waste treatment plant and system operators remove harmful pollutants from liquid waste so that it is safe to return to the environment. High school diploma is required, and associate's degree or one-year certificate in water quality and liquid waste treatment technology is preferred. Certification is required to oversee various treatment processes, and some states may have additional requirements. Coursework in math, chemistry, and biology is helpful. Computer literacy and mechanical skills are essential to manage computerized systems. Operators must have good organizational and problem-solving skills. It is important to have knowledge of federal and state environmental and water-related laws, and critical to keep current with amendments and industry issues.

Salary Range: $31,380 to $32,635.

☞ *Inside Track:* Maintaining clean, safe water and adhering to strict federal and state regulations will spur demand for qualified operators in local governments, private water supply, and sanitary service companies. Increased pretreatment of water by manufacturing firms and building of new plants to meet growing population also will create new job opportunities. Job seekers with postsecondary degree or higher education will have best opportunities, as companies seek candidates to handle the complexities of meeting drinking water and water pollution standards.

MEDIA AND THE ARTS

Actors, Producers, and Directors
Advertising, Marketing, Promotions, and Sales Managers
Artists
Broadcast and Sound Engineering Technicians and
	Radio Operators
Graphic Designers
Photographers
Public Relations Specialists
Television, Video, and Motion Picture Camera Operators
	and Editors
Writers and Editors

ACTORS, PRODUCERS, AND DIRECTORS

Job Skills and Requirements: Actors, producers, and directors express ideas and tell stories in film, radio, television, and theater. College degree and experience in performing arts are preferred. For actors, local and regional theater experience and summer stock will help build skills and resume. Raw talent, creativity, passion for the arts, and an unrelentless drive to succeed are important in this highly competitive field. Unless you're a highly-paid star, most actors must be willing to supplement income by working odd jobs while pursuing craft. Directors must have training, experience, and creativity, and must know intricacies of technical equipment and processes that go into moviemaking, including cameras, lighting, and editing. Producers need strong business acumen and solid entrepreneurial, negotiating, and marketing skills to oversee business and financial side of production.

Salary Ranges: Actors $25,920 to $26,957.
Producers and directors $41,030 to $42,671.

☞ *Inside Track:* Generating demand for actors, producers, and directors are expanding cable and satellite television operations and increasing production and distribution of major studio and independent films. In addition, a significant rise in interactive media and moviemaking and videomaking for the Web will spur growth. Despite good outlook, competition for acting jobs is stiff in major cities, particularly New York City and Los Angeles. Actors will find more opportunities in the leisure industry, including resort areas, cruise lines, and theme parks that entertain guests with shows. Actors should be listed with a casting agency and join the Screen Actors Guild or other professional organizations.

ADVERTISING, MARKETING, PROMOTIONS, AND SALES MANAGERS

Job Skills and Requirements: Advertising, marketing, promotions, and sales managers direct the sale of products and services and coordinate activities, including market research and strategy. Bachelor's or master's degree is required. Coursework in sociology, psychology, literature, journalism, advertising, marketing, and business administration is helpful as is knowledge of consumer behavior, market research, sales and communications. With rapid growth in interactive advertising and marketing, computer and visual communication skills are essential. Strong analytical capabilities and good judgment are important, as well as ability to communicate effectively in writing and speaking. Creative business mind and solid team-building skills are essential.

Salary Ranges: Advertising and promotions managers $53,360 to $55,495.
Marketing managers $71,240 to $74,090.
Sales managers $68,520 to $71,260.

☞ *Inside Track:* As global competition intensifies, businesses are requiring greater marketing, promotions, and advertising to make consumers aware of products and services. Job growth is expected to rise much faster than average in most business services industries, such as computer and data processing, and in management and public relations firms. Job seekers with college degree, experience, and strong communication skills will have competitive edge. Must be willing to work long hours, including weekends, and work well under pressure to meet deadlines. Jobs may involve extensive travel to meet with clients. Proven industry track record will provide competitive edge.

ARTISTS

Job Skills and Requirements: Artists, including illustrators and multimedia artists and animators, use creativity to communicate ideas. Bachelor's or master's degree in fine arts is required. Ability to sketch by freehand is essential, and solid multimedia computer software skills are critical. Medical illustrators must have demonstrated artistic ability and a detailed knowledge of human and animal anatomy; a bachelor's or master's degree combining art and premedical courses is preferred. Artists must demonstrate strong creative flair and effectively communicate ideas, thoughts, and feelings visually. Important to keep current with cutting-edge computer and multimedia technologies.

Salary Range: Multimedia artists and animators $41,130 to $42,775.

☞ *Inside Track:* Visual communications are increasingly important as a key component of booming Internet and communications media industries. Job opportunities for illustrators, cartoonists, and animators will generate from growing entertainment industry, including computer games, cable, and motion picture production. Companies increasingly will seek artistic talent to make web sites and products more visually appealing. More than half of all artists are self-employed. Most others work in computer software, printing, advertising, and design firms. Candidates with strong portfolios demonstrating range of skills and creative talent will have competitive edge.

BROADCAST AND SOUND ENGINEERING TECHNICIANS AND RADIO OPERATORS

Job Skills and Requirements: Broadcast and sound engineering technicians and radio operators install, test, repair, and operate electronic-based media equipment, such as microphones and television cameras. Formal training in broadcast technology, engineering, or electronics from a technical school or community college is required. Coursework in math, physics, and electronics is helpful. Hands-on experience is vital in order to learn business and hone skills. Gaining experience in small television or radio stations will provide edge in applying for jobs in larger stations in major cities. Certification by the Society of Broadcast Engineers is important. Technicians must have basic computer skills and flexibility to perform a variety of duties. Good manual dexterity is necessary, as well as aptitude to work with electronic, electrical, and mechanical systems and equipment.

Salary Ranges: Broadcast technicians $26,950 to $28,028.
Sound engineering technicians $39,480 to $41,060.
Radio operators $29,260 to $30,430.

☞ *Inside Track:* Job openings are projected to grow due to the rising number of programming hours required by 24-hour cable television and radio stations. As broadcast stations migrate from analog to digital, technicians who can install transmitters will be in high demand. Employment of technicians and operators also is projected to grow significantly in the cable industry, where businesses will need to install and maintain new audio and visual technologies to stay competitive, such as cable modems that deliver high-speed Internet access to personal computers and digital set-top boxes. Also spurring job growth are the number of experienced technicians and operators who leave the field for jobs in other areas, including computer or industrial repair.

GRAPHIC DESIGNERS

Job Skills and Requirements: Graphic designers combine artistic ability and practical knowledge to turn abstract ideas into formal designs for products. Bachelor's degree is required and master's degree will provide competitive edge. It is critical to sketch by hand and to have solid computer-aided design (CAD) skills. Creativity, artistic flair, and imagination are necessary. Graphic designers must have a strong eye for color and detail, and must effectively communicate ideas in a variety of mediums. The ability to use a variety of print, electronic, and film mediums to create designs that meet clients' commercial needs is important. It is essential to have good problem-solving skills and be able to work well independently and under pressure of deadlines. It is important to stay current with cultural trends and be open to new ideas and diverse tastes.

Salary Range: $34,570 to $35,953.

☞ *Inside Track:* Strong demand for graphic designers is expected because of companies' increasing need for compelling Web-based graphics for Internet sites, videos, presentations, and promotional materials. Growth in the entertainment industry will also generate demand for designers to work on television, video, movie, and Internet graphics. Candidates with artistic flair, experience, college degree, and strong portfolio will have best opportunities. Graphic designers must keep current with computer technology involving layout and design for Web pages, magazines, and other publications and for signage, marketing brochures, and promotional displays.

PHOTOGRAPHERS

Job Skills and Requirements: Photographers produce and preserve images that record events. Technical expertise and creativity are required to produce commercial-quality photographs. Formal training at vocational school is required, and bachelor's degree in photojournalism or communications is preferred. Coursework in equipment, processes, techniques, and design is helpful. Photographers must have good eyesight, an eye for color and design, artistic ability, and manual dexterity. They must be patient, willing to take risks, and pay close attention to details. With digital photography and computer-based imagery rapidly expanding, it is critical to have strong computer skills in related software programs. Freelancers must know how to promote business, prepare business contracts, hire assistants, and secure copyright protection for work.

Salary Range: $22,300 to $23,192.

☞ *Inside Track:* Demand for photographers is growing from increasing need for high-quality digital photos for web sites and for electronic versions of magazines, newspapers, and journals. Portrait photographers are projected to have job growth from rising population, and commercial and industrial photographers will be in demand for photographing buildings, landmarks, and products for manuals, reports, advertisements, and catalogs. Photographers employed in government or advertising agencies typically work five-day, 40-hour weeks. Most photographers, however, work long, irregular hours, and must be available to work on short notice.

PUBLIC RELATIONS SPECIALISTS

Job Skills and Requirements: Public relations specialists create positive images and serve as advocates for organizations. Bachelor's degree and public relations experience, typically gained through internships, are required. Coursework in public relations, journalism, advertising, and interpersonal communications is helpful. Excellent grammar, writing, and editing skills are important. The ability to communicate effectively in writing and speaking is critical. Computer skills are necessary to create presentations and prepare documents. Creativity, pleasant personality, and good judgment are essential. It is important to have discretion and good decision-making and problem-solving skills.

Salary Range: $39,580 to $41,163.

☞ *Inside Track:* Organizations increasingly will need good public relations to promote and protect their images in order to stay competitive. Best opportunities will be for job seekers with college degrees and hands-on experience. Having a portfolio of writing samples and published works also will provide edge. Employment in public relations firms will grow, as more businesses seek contract work on a project-to-project basis. Job opportunities typically will be concentrated in large cities, where many public relations firms and corporate headquarters are located. Work can be demanding, especially during a crisis. It is important to maintain good relationships with public and media. Memberships in local chapters of the Public Relations Society of America or the International Association of Business Communicators provide job seekers with places to network with industry professionals.

TELEVISION, VIDEO, AND MOTION PICTURE CAMERA OPERATORS AND EDITORS

Job Skills and Requirements: Operators and editors produce images that tell a story, inform, or entertain an audience. Formal training in videography and camera operation is required from postsecondary school or university. Basic courses in lights, cameras, equipment, processes, and techniques are essential. Solid knowledge of technical and computer-based equipment is critical. Artistic ability and good hand-eye coordination are necessary. Camera operators must be patient, accurate, and have good eye for detail. They must be willing to travel, carry heavy equipment, and stand for long periods of time holding a camera.

Salary Range: $27,870 to $28,985.

☞ *Inside Track:* Rapid expansion in the motion picture and entertainment, computer, and Internet industries will be spurring strong job growth for camera operators and editors. Camera operators will be in demand to film made-for-Internet broadcasts, including music videos and live concerts, digital movies, sports events, and entertainment programming. Job seekers who are highly motivated, have excellent technical skills, and can adapt to changing technologies will have edge. For freelancers, new business is often acquired through referrals from past projects, so it is important to develop good relationships with coworkers and have good reputations in industry. Many camera operators who work in film or video are freelancers, and good opportunities are expected in cable television. Job seekers should subscribe to trade publications to keep current with industry trends.

WRITERS AND EDITORS

Job Skills and Requirements: Writers communicate through words, and editors prepare materials for publication or broadcast. Bachelor's or master's degree in liberal arts, communications, journalism, or English is required. Technical writing requires degree in or knowledge of specialized field, such as engineering, medicine or science. Solid grammar and punctuation and strong command of the English language are critical. It is important to have computer software skills to compose and edit, and essential to be able to express ideas clearly and logically and to demonstrate good judgment and ethics. Creativity and self-discipline are important. Curious and inquisitive mind is necessary during research, and a writer or editor must fact-check and produce accurate work on deadline.

Salary Ranges: Writers $42,270 to $43,960.
Technical writers $47,790 to $49,702.
Editors $39,370 to $40,945.

☞ *Inside Track:* There will be more job prospects for writers and editors, as organizations develop and publish their own newsletters and Internet sites. In addition, increased demand for writers to produce content for Internet sites and for special-interest magazines will spur significant job growth. Advertising and public relations agencies also will seek talented writers and editors to meet clients' needs. More technical writers with expertise, such as law, medicine, and technology, will be needed to translate technical information into reader-friendly materials. Rapid change in technology and electronics industry will also generate greater need for writers to compose users' guides, instruction manuals, and training materials. Job seekers who have good computer software skills, a creative flair, and solid grammar, punctuation, writing, and editing skills will have competitive edge. A portfolio of writing samples showing range of writing styles also will be advantageous.

SALES AND PROFESSIONAL SERVICES

Animal Care and Service Workers
Cashiers
Cosmetologists and Personal Appearance Workers
Retail Salespersons

ANIMAL CARE AND SERVICE WORKERS

Job Skills and Requirements: Animal care and service workers, including caretakers, groomers, and trainers, take care of pets' needs. High school diploma is required. Most skills are acquired on the job. Groomers must complete an apprenticeship or training program. For animal trainers, some employers may require bachelor's degree in biology, zoology, or related field. Love of animals is important, and workers must be sensitive, patient, and gentle with pets.

Salary Ranges: Caretakers $15,954 to $16,592.
Trainers $21,923 to $22,800.

☞ *Inside Track:* The growing popularity of house pets, specifically dogs and cats, will spur growth in grooming services, daily and overnight boarding, and training. Job growth for trainer will generate from an increased number of animal owners seeking specialized pet training to modify cat's or dog's behavior. Caretakers also will find opportunities in animal shelters. Although no formal education is required, job seekers with certified training courses in grooming and kennel care will have more opportunities. Training programs and workshops are available through the Humane Society of the United States, the American Humane Association, and the National Animal Control Association. The American Boarding Kennels Association offers a home-study program in pet care.

CASHIERS

Job Skills and Requirements: Cashiers work computer-based machines to accept payment for customers' purchase of goods or services. High school diploma is preferred, and most employers train on the job. Must have good basic math skills and familiarity with typing. Because cashiers handle large amounts of cash, they must be trustworthy and honest. Good customer service skills are essential in order to interact with public and represent business well.

Salary Range: $14,456 to $15,034.

☞ *Inside Track:* Cashiers, who typically work in supermarkets, department stores, convenience stores, and other service industries, will have significant job opportunities over the next decade, as the growing population is generating more goods and services and more customer service needs. In some businesses, such as supermarkets, cashiers may have other responsibilities, including stocking shelves. This will be one of the occupations with the most openings, and candidates who are dependable, trustworthy, and have good personalities will have the best opportunities.

COSMETOLOGISTS AND PERSONAL APPEARANCE WORKERS

Job Skills and Requirements: Cosmetologists, including hairstylists, manicurists, pedicurists, and skin care specialists, provide beauty services to clients. All states require cosmetologists and most other personal appearance workers to be state licensed, but qualifications vary. Formal training program in cosmetology at vocational school is required. Many states require separate licensing exams for manicurists, pedicurists, and skin care specialists. Knowledge of fashion, art, and technical design is important, and it is critical to have superior customer service skills and an outgoing personality to interact with clients and ensure repeat customers. Finger dexterity, sense of form and artistry, and desire to help people look more attractive are important. Cosmetologists must enjoy working with people, be flexible about following clients' directions, keep up-to-date on latest fashion and beauty trends, and be willing to work long hours, evenings, and weekends.

Salary Range: $17,660 to $18,366.

☞ *Inside Track:* As the population rises and more people demand luxury services, demand will be strong for personal appearance workers, particularly for manicurists, pedicurists, hairstylists, and colorists. Rapid growth in the number of nail salons and full-service day spas also will generate numerous job openings. Opportunities will be best for cosmetologists licensed in a broad range of services and for candidates who have superior people skills.

RETAIL SALESPERSONS

Job Skills and Requirements: Sales representatives use sales techniques to assist customers and encourage purchases. High school diploma is preferred, and training typically is on the job. Knowledge of products is important in order to assist customers with questions, and certain products, such as cosmetics, may require specialized training sessions. A salesperson must have excellent customer service skills, a pleasant personality, and professional appearance, and maintain a patient, calm demeanor when dealing with irate customers. It is important to be courteous, efficient, and enjoy helping people. A salesperson must have flexibility with work schedule, as hours typically include evenings, weekends, and holidays.

Salary Range: $16,681 to $17,348.

☞ *Inside Track:* One of the occupations with the most openings, retail salesperson jobs will be plentiful over the next decade to replace the large number of workers who leave the occupation each year, as well as to meet the growing population's demand for good customer service. Businesses increasingly will need top-notch customer service to remain competitive, so best opportunities will be for candidates with excellent people and sales skills. To move into supervisory or management positions, associate's degree in retail sales or bachelor's degree is essential. The largest employers of retail salespersons are department stores, clothing and accessories stores, furniture stores, and car dealers.

SCIENCE

Biological and Medical Scientists
Chemists and Materials Scientists
Environmental Scientists and Geologists
Physicists and Astronomers
Science Technicians

BIOLOGICAL AND MEDICAL SCIENTISTS

Job Skills and Requirements: Biological and medical scientists study living organisms and their relationship to the environment. Master's degree in applied research or product development is required, but Ph.D. is required for independent research. Medical scientists who administer certain techniques to drug or gene patients must have a Ph.D. and a medical degree. It is helpful to have courses in chemistry, biology, physics, and math, and critical to have strong computer skills and knowledge of computerized laboratory equipment. Scientists must be able to work well both independently and with a team and be able to communicate findings both verbally and in writing. Scientists who want to work in management or administrative positions should have strong business administration skills and be familiar with regulatory issues and management techniques.

Salary Range: $49,239 to $51,208.

☞ *Inside Track:* Job outlook will be good for scientists over the next decade, resulting from new advancements in biotechnology and gene therapies, which require further study to take research to the next level. Pharmaceutical companies are expected to increasingly use biotechnology techniques, and more research will be conducted for health-related issues, including AIDS, cancer, and Alzheimer's disease. In addition, efforts to discover new ways to improve the environment also will spur job growth. Candidates with master's degree in biological science will have best edge in nonresearch positions, and the number of science-related jobs in sales, marketing, and research management is expected to grow significantly. Most employment is in local and federal governments and in pharmaceutical and biotechnology companies, research labs, and hospitals.

CHEMISTS AND MATERIALS SCIENTISTS

Job Skills and Requirements: Chemists and materials scientists research and study structures and chemical compounds of various materials to develop products. Bachelor's degree in chemistry, materials science, or physics is required, but Ph.D. is necessary for research and development positions. Courses in science, math, physics, and inorganic, organic, and physical chemistry are helpful. Computer knowledge is critical, and knowledge of business, marketing, and economics is important. Chemists must be patient, dedicated, detail-oriented, and disciplined, and must have strong communication skills to present findings and interact with team members and other professionals.

Salary Range: $50,080 to $52,083.

☞ *Inside Track:* As competition intensifies among drug companies, job growth is expected to rise in pharmaceutical and biotechnology companies and in research and testing services firms. Chemists and scientists will be needed to develop new and better pharmaceuticals and personal care products, as well as more breakthrough drugs to attack diseases. Biotechnological research, including gene study, also is a powerful driver of job growth. Chemical firms that develop personal products such as toiletries and cosmetics need to hire highly skilled workers to continually develop new products in order to stay competitive in the marketplace. Best opportunities will be for chemists with master's degree or Ph.D.

ENVIRONMENTAL SCIENTISTS AND GEOLOGISTS

Job Skills and Requirements: Environmental scientists conduct research to identify and help eliminate sources of pollutants that affect people, wildlife, and the environment. Geologists study the composition and structure of the earth. Bachelor's degree in geology, environmental engineering, or hydrogeology is required, but master's degree is preferred. Ph.D. is required for research positions in universities or government. Coursework in hydrology, chemistry, hazardous waste management, and environmental legislation is helpful. It is critical to have good computer skills, particularly in data analysis, digital mapping, remote sensing, and geographic information systems, and important to have knowledge of the Global Positioning System, a locator system that uses satellites. Some employers seek scientists with field and laboratory experience. Must work well independently and as part of team. Strong communication skills are important in order to write technical reports, produce research proposals, and explain findings to others. Must be inquisitive, have good problem-solving abilities, and deeply care about the environment.

Salary Range: $44,180 to $45,947.

☞ *Inside Track:* The increasing need for companies to comply with environmental laws and regulations will spur demand for environmental scientists and geoscientists, especially those who specialize in hydrogeology and engineering. Issues of water conservation, deteriorating coasts, and rising populations in more environmentally sensitive locations will generate job opportunities. Scientists who are knowledgeable in both science and engineering aspects of waste remediation will have edge in the marketplace, as scientists will be needed to conduct research on hazardous waste sites. Increasing highway and interstate construction also will stimulate job growth. About one out of three scientists work in engineering and management services, while others are employed by oil and gas extraction firms, metal mining companies, or the federal government.

PHYSICISTS AND ASTRONOMERS

Job Skills and Requirements: Physicists explore and identify the principles governing the structure and behavior of matter and energy. Astronomers use the principles of physics and mathematics to learn about the solar system. Doctoral degree is required for best jobs, including teaching, research, and study of the universe. Background in lasers, cyclotrons, telescopes, mass spectrometers, and other high-tech equipment is necessary, as is knowledge of physical laws and theories to problems in nuclear energy, aerospace technology, and navigation equipment.

Strong math, problem-solving, and analytical skills are essential. Physicists who strive to work in industrial laboratories should also take courses in economics and business management. Imagination and initiative are important, and strong communication skills are critical to effectively discuss findings in research papers and in verbal presentations.

Salary Range: $82,535 to $85,836.

☞ *Inside Track:* Because federal defense expenditures will increase over the next decade, good job growth is projected, particularly to replace retiring physicists and astronomers. Physicists and astronomers also will be in high demand for computer software development and in areas of information and semiconductor technologies. Nearly half of all physicists and astronomers work for commercial or noncommercial research, development, and testing laboratories. The federal government employs about 35 percent, mostly in the U.S. Department of Defense. Foreign language is helpful if you work abroad.

SCIENCE TECHNICIANS

Job Skills and Requirements: Science technicians use scientific and mathematical theories and principles to solve problems in research and development. Associate's degree in applied science is required, and some employers may require bachelor's degree in chemistry, biology, or forensic science. Experience in laboratories is helpful. Strong computer and technical skills are necessary in order to operate and maintain lab instruments, monitor experiments, and calculate and record results. It is critical to have attention to detail to keep logs of work activities. Technicians must be able to work independently and be willing to work under direction of scientist.

Salary Range: $35,464 to $36,883.

☞ *Inside Track:* Job prospects are excellent for science technicians to meet chemical and drug companies' growing demand for new and improved pharmaceuticals and personal care products. Need for science technicians in the environmental field is growing, as more work is being done to regulate waste products and to protect air, water, and soil. Job opportunities will be best for skilled graduates of science technician training programs. Employers will be seeking well-trained candidates who have highly developed technical and communication skills to manage complexities of research and development.

RECOMMENDED READING

Ahlricks, Nancy S. *Competing for Talent: Key Recruitment and Retention Strategies for Becoming an Employer of Choice*. Palo Alto, CA: Davies-Black Publishing, 2000.

Bell, Ella L. J. Edmondson, and Stella M. Nkomo. *Our Separate Ways: Black and White Women and the Struggle for Professional Identity*. Boston: Harvard Business School, 2001.

Bernbach, Jeffrey M. *Job Discrimination II: How to Fight, How to Win*. Englewood Cliffs, NJ: Voir Dire Press, 1998.

Branham, F. Leigh. *Keeping the People Who Keep You in Business*. New York: AMACOM, 2000.

Chambers, Harry E. *Effective Communication Skills for Scientific and Technical Professionals*. New York: Perseus Books, 2000.

Ciulla, Joanne B. *The Working Life: The Promise and Betrayal of Modern Work*. New York: Three Rivers Press, 2001.

Dobson, Michael S., and Deborah Singer Dobson. *Managing Up: 59 Ways to Build a Career-Advancing Relationship with Your Boss*. New York: AMACOM, 1999.

Franklin, Stephen, and William Serrin. *Three Strikes*. New York: Guilford Press, 2001.

Fraser, Jill Andresky. *White Collar Sweatshop: The Deterioration of Work and Its Rewards in Corporate America*. New York: W.W. Norton & Co., 2001.

Germer, Fawn. *Hard Won Wisdom: More than 50 Extraordinary Women Mentor You to Find Self-Awareness, Perspective, and Balance*. New York: Perigee, 2001.

Gibson, Karon White, Patricia Skalka, and Joy Smith Catterson. *Nurses on Our Own.* Campbell, CA: iUniverse, 2000.

Gordon, Gil E. *Turn It Off: How to Unplug from the Anytime-Anywhere Office without Disconnecting Your Career.* New York: Three Rivers Press, 2001.

Greenberg, Herbert M. *How to Hire and Develop Your Next Top Performer.* New York: McGraw-Hill, 2000.

Hoefling, Trina. *Working Virtually.* Dylles, WA: Stylus, 2001.

Hubbartt, William S. *The New Battle over Workplace Privacy.* New York: AMACOM, 1998.

Kenig, Graciela. *Best Careers for Bilingual Latinos.* New York: McGraw-Hill, 1998.

Kleiman, Carol. *The Career Coach.* Chicago: Dearborn Financial Publishing, 1994.

Kleiman, Carol. *Getting a Job: Your Shortcut to Success!* New York: John Wiley & Sons, 2000.

Kleiman, Carol. *The 100 Best Jobs for the 1990s and Beyond.* New York: Berkley Books, 1994.

Maxey, Cyndi, and Barry Lyerly. *Training from the Heart.* Alexandria, VA: American Society for Training and Development, 2000.

Meyerson, Debra E. *Tempered Radicals: How People Use Difference to Inspire Change at Work.* Boston: Harvard Business School Press, 2001.

Monthly Labor Review Online. Washington, DC: U.S. Department of Labor, Bureau of Labor Statistics, 2001–2002.

Nash, Linda. *The Bounce Back Quotient.* St. Louis: Prism Publications, 2000.

Newman, Betsy Kyte. *Getting Unstuck: Moving Ahead with Your Career.* Boston: Pearson Custom Publishing, 2000.

Nickles, Liz. *The Change Agents: Decoding the New Work Force and the New Workplace.* New York: St. Martin's Press, 2001.

Occupational Outlook Handbook, 2002–03 Edition. Washington, DC: U.S. Department of Labor, Bureau of Labor Statistics, 2002.

Otterbourg, Robert K. *Switching Careers.* Washington, DC: Kiplinger Books, 2001.

Purmal, Kate, and Chris Bennett. *Strong Voices, Real Choices: Professional Women Speak Out about Their Choice to Work Less.* Danville, CA: WorkVantage, 2001.

Reich, Robert B. *The Future of Success: Working and Living in the New Economy.* New York: Vintage Books, 2002.

Repa, Barbara Kate. *Your Rights in the Workplace.* Berkeley: Nolo Press, 1999.

Rocks, Celia. *Organizing the Good Life: A Path to Joyful Simplicity—Home to Work and Back.* Facts on Demand Press, 2001.

Roehm, Frances E., and Margaret Riley Dikel. *The Guide to Internet Job Searching.* Chicago: Contemporary Books, 2002.

Russell, Toni. *Malignant Personalities: Protecting Yourself in the Workplace.* Campbell, CA: iUniverse, 2000.

Solovic, Susan Wilson. *The Girl's Guide to Power and Success.* New York: AMACOM, 2001.

Thomas, R. Roosevelt, Jr. *Building a House for Diversity.* New York: AMACOM, 1999.

Tobias, Paul, and Susan Sauter. *Job Rights and Survival Strategies: A Handbook for Terminated Employees.* Cincinnati: National Employee Rights Institute, 1997.

Tulgan, Bruce, and Carolyn Martin. *Managing Generation Y.* Amherst, MA: Human Resource Development Press, 2001.

Viscusi, Stephen. *On the Job: How to Make It in the Real World of Work.* New York: Three Rivers Press, 2001.

Wackerle, Frederick W., and William W. George. *The Right CEO: Straight Talk about Making Tough CEO Selection Decisions.* San Francisco: Jossey-Bass, 2001.

Waldroop, James, and Timothy Butler. *The 12 Bad Habits That Hold Good People Back: Overcoming the Behavior Patterns That Keep You from Getting Ahead.* New York: Doubleday, 2001.

Wellington, Sheila. *Be Your Own Mentor: Strategies from Top Women on the Secrets of Success.* New York: Random House, 2001.

White, Jennifer. *Work Less, Make More.* New York: John Wiley & Sons, 1999.

INDEX

Printed in the United States
34176LVS00003B/45

9 780471 235255